Sebastian Keen

Manual of Devotions

In honour of the seven dolours of the Blessed Virgin Mary. Second Edition

Sebastian Keen

Manual of Devotions
In honour of the seven dolours of the Blessed Virgin Mary. Second Edition

ISBN/EAN: 9783337299965

Printed in Europe, USA, Canada, Australia, Japan

Cover: Foto ©Lupo / pixelio.de

More available books at **www.hansebooks.com**

MANUAL OF DEVOTIONS

IN HONOUR OF

THE SEVEN DOLOURS

OF THE

BLESSED VIRGIN MARY.

BY

FATHER SEBASTIAN

Of the Blessed Sacrament,

Religious of the Congregation of the Cross and Passion of Our Lord Jesus Christ.

DEVOUTLY DEDICATED TO
The Immaculate Heart of the Queen of the Sorrowful.

Second Edition

LONDON:
DENIS LANE, PRINTER AND PUBLISHER, 310, STRAND.
1868.

INDEX.

	PAGE.
PREFACE	1

PART I.

Reflections on the Seven Dolours.

ON THE FIRST DOLOUR OF MARY.
Holy Simeon foretells the sorrows of Mary.... 7

ON THE SECOND DOLOUR.
Mary's flight into Egypt..................... 24

ON THE THIRD DOLOUR.
Mary loses Jesus for Three Days 42

ON THE FOURTH DOLOUR.
Mary meets her Divine Son bearing his Cross to Calvary................................ 60

ON THE FIFTH DOLOUR.
Mary beholds the Crucifixion of Jesus........ 76

ON THE SIXTH DOLOUR.

	PAGE
The dead body of Jesus is placed upon the arms of Mary	93

ON THE SEVENTH DOLOUR.

Mary at the Burial of Jesus	109

PART II.

Devout Prayers in honour of the Seven Dolours	124
Rosary of the Seven Dolours	128
Litany of the Seven Dolours	132
Memorare Triste	137
The Way of the Mother; in the same form as the Way of the Cross	138
Short Method of Meditating on the Seven Dolours	162
OF THE SCAPULAR AND ROSARY OF THE SEVEN DOLOURS	164
Historical Sketch of ditto	*ibid.*
Obligations and practices of piety of ditto	170
Formula for blessing ditto	175

	PAGE.

Devotion of Saint Paul of the Cross towards the Seven Dolours 181
Commemoration of the Seven Dolours........ 189
Litany of our Lady of Sorrows.............. 195
Lamentation of Mary at the Foot of the Cross 199
Hymns for the Feast of the Seven Dolours 204
A Novena in honour of the Seven Dolours 208
Mass of the Seven Dolours (Latin and English) 215
Stabat Mater (Latin and English) 230
St. Bonaventura's Short Office of the Seven Dolours 281
Rule of Life................................ 318
The Month of Devotion to the Suffering Heart of Mary................................ 324
The Month of the Seven Dolours 326
Indulgences: pp. 127, 130, 139, 164, 172, 195, 213, 326 327

TO THE PIOUS READER.

A dutiful child, beloved reader, is never unmindful of the sorrows of his mother. Her sighs and labours are ever deeply imprinted on his memory, and he is bent on fulfilling that sacred command of Heaven which venerable Tobias gave to his faithful son:—" Thou must be mindful what and how great were the perils which thy mother suffered for thee;" and which Ecclesiasticus, inspired by the Holy Ghost, gives to all mankind, in these words: "Forget not the groanings of thy mother."

As Christians, we are all children

of Mary. She became our Mother amidst unutterable anguish and pain. She was solemnly declared our Mother when standing at the foot of the Cross, whilst the blood flowed in streams from the wounds of her dying Jesus. For our loving Redeemer, being about to leave this world, and pitying our orphan state, addressed every Christian, in the person of St. John, his beloved disciple—"Behold thy Mother:" then, turning his bleeding head towards the Blessed Virgin, He said, as the same Evangelist testifies—"Woman behold thy Son." We, therefore, are the children of Mary: Jesus has declared us such. "As Christ has begotten us," says St. Antoninus, "to a spiritual life, in the word of truth, by suffering on the cross, so, likewise, Mary has begotten us, and brought us forth in the midst of most acute pains, by sharing in the sufferings of the crucifixion of her Son." Ah, then, never let us forget her sighs and groans—her bitter pains and sorrows. Deeply should we fix them in our memory, and day after day call them to mind.

"Forget not the groanings of thy Mother, and be mindful what and how great were the perils which she suffered for thee." In order to assist you in so doing, dear reader, I present you with a few reflections on each of Mary's Dolours, convinced that, if you meditate on them often, you will imitate her virtues, share in her merits, and obtain her special protection.

But that you, my dear reader, may be still more encouraged to think of the

Seven Dolours, let me remind you of some other advantages which you will gain from this most beautiful and consoling devotion.

It was revealed to St. Elizabeth, a Benedictine nun, that our Lord will bestow four graces on those who are devout to the sorrows of the Blessed Virgin. First, that whoever invokes her by her Dolours, shall obtain the grace of true repentance. Secondly, that she will console such in all their tribulations, and especially at the hour of death. Thirdly, that the Lord will imprint on their minds a remembrance of his Passion, and inspire them with great devotion to it. Lastly, that He has empowered Mary to obtain for them whatever blessings she pleases.

The following striking example, revealed to St. Bridget, will greatly confirm the promises made to St. Elizabeth. She narrates that there was a certain nobleman, who had bound himself by compact to Satan for sixty years, and had during that time led a very criminal life; that before his death he obtained forgiveness, because he felt compassion for the Blessed Virgin whenever he heard the Dolours mentioned.

Therefore, I present this little book of Mary's sorrows. Receive it with affection, and peruse it attentively; and as the bee, when it lights upon a flower, does not leave it until it has gathered all the honey that flower affords, so if you meet with anything which may touch or move your heart, dwell upon that until you have derived from it all the profit you can. Trusting that this my first humble effort will not have been in vain, I commend you, dear reader, and these Devotions in honour of the Seven Dolours, to the maternal heart of Mary—simply repeating to you what the heavenly voice said to St. Augustine, "Tolle lege, tolle lege."—"Take up and read, take up and read."

Feast of the Seven Dolours,
1867.

PART THE FIRST.

REFLECTIONS ON THE SEVEN DOLOURS.

ON THE FIRST DOLOUR OF MARY.

Holy Simeon foretells the Sorrows of Mary.

FIRST POINT.

The law of God, given by Moses to the Jews, ordained that a woman, after childbirth, should undergo the ceremonies of Purification. For a certain time she was forbidden to appear in public, nor was she allowed to touch anything which was consecrated to the worship of the Most High. Besides this law of purification, we read in Leviticus of another law, which ordained that every first-born son should be offered to God, and, after his presentation, ransomed for a specified sum of money. Now, observe that Mary was not bound to fulfil either of these laws. As regards the first, certainly it could not oblige her; since it supposed defilement in the person to be purified. But in Mary there was no stain; she was ever a most pure virgin, as even many enemies of our holy faith admit. Moreover, we know from the second chapter of St. Luke, that Jesus was conceived in her sacred womb by the power of the Holy Ghost.

Hence, our Blessed Lady was by no means bound to undergo any ceremony of purification. Again, one of the offerings made on the day of purification was a pigeon or a dove, to be sacrificed for sin. But what sin was there in Mary? Was it original sin? No! Because from her inviolate womb the Son of God Himself took that hallowed flesh with which He clothed his divine nature. Hence the holy fathers declare, and the Church teaches as an article of faith, that she was immaculate in and from her conception. Nor did she ever contaminate her soul by the slightest defilement of actual sin.

On her lips there was no deceit—in her heart no guile—in her soul no imperfection. Gabriel, the archangel, solemnly declared that she was "full of grace." The Blessed Virgin, therefore, was not bound by the Levitical law, enacted for all other mothers in Israel.

Nor was she obliged to fulfil the law of presentation: first, because her Son being truly God, and therefore the very author of the law, was not subject to his own law. God is bound by no precept which He has given to his creatures; much less by one which requires his own redemption. Secondly, Mary was not bound by this law, because her Son, being a Divine Person, was one God with the Eternal Father and the Holy Ghost, and therefore needed no dedication.

But, though Mary knew well that these two laws, commanded by Moses, did not regard her, nevertheless she faithfully and exactly fulfilled both. For when the required days of retirement were completed, carrying in her arms the infant Jesus, she hastened to the Temple, accompanied by St. Joseph, taking with her a pair of turtle doves, which were sanctioned by the law as a sufficient offering for very poor persons.

Behold now the Mother of God on her way to Jerusalem, for the purpose of performing the rites of presentation and purification. One perfectly immaculate goes to the Temple as though, like other daughters of sinful Eve, she required to be cleansed. What an excellent lesson of humility for us is here! Mary places herself in the position of a sinner. She boasts not of the sublime dignity of her sacred maternity. She tells not the people that she is the daughter of the Eternal Father —the Virgin Mother of the Omnipotent Son—and the Spouse of the Holy Ghost. Nor does she on account of these exalted relationships, plead exemption from the humiliating laws.

How different is my conduct! If by God's mercy I enjoy any privileges, I take great pains to manifest them; and often, to the prejudice of others, I lose no opportunity of making it known that I possess them. As for being considered worse than I am, it is the object of all my efforts to avoid it—nay, I even wish to be esteemed better than I am. I wish to be looked on by all as clean of heart, while the disgusting leprosy of sin defiles my soul. I would have others think me just, while, in the all-seeing Eye of Infinite Sanctity, I am a very great sinner. O foul, O miserable pride, truly thou art the principal cause of my spiritual ruin!

Therefore, from the Blessed Virgin's purification let me learn holy humility: I will devoutly beseech her to obtain for me this foundation of all virtues, without which it is in vain that I aspire to please God, or to be a sharer of that heavenly bliss, promised to the just. For our Divine Lord has said: "Whosoever shall exalt himself shall be humbled, and he that shall humble himself shall be exalted."

St. Bernard says of our Blessed Lady, "As no creature ever went down so deep into the abyss of humility, so no

She was content that He should die, for the glory of God and the salvation of the world. Together with this sacrifice of her innocent Son, she humbly offered up her heart, praying the Eternal Father to afflict it according to his Divine pleasure. Her sole delight was in the fulfilment of his most holy will. Taulerus says that our Blessed Lady did not regard the sword of agony which was to lacerate her heart—that she did not reflect on the most precious treasure she was to lose—nor did she take into consideration how she was to be completely deprived of all joy, happiness and her most loveable Son; but she resigned herself with her every faculty to the most adorable will of God, prepared to accept every burden, every affliction, and all the most grievous tortures of soul which might come upon her through those afflictions. Ah, heavenly resignation of Mary's heart! When shall I begin, in my poor degree, to imitate her patience and submission?

"To understand the supernatural victory which Mary achieved in the oblation of this sacrifice," says the great St. Alphonsus, "it is necessary to know the nature of her love for Jesus. She was his mother. Now, maternal love is in general so strong that when a child is at the point of death, and the mother about to lose him, she forgets his defects and any uneasiness she may have suffered on his account, and feels pain beyond expression at the thought of being separated from him. But the love of mothers for the most part is divided among their children. Not so was it with Mary; she had but one Son, and He the most beautiful and excellent of all the children of Adam—loveable, obedient, virtuous, and innocent in his own supereminent degree—yea, more —her God and her all." How great, then, and how heroic was Mary's resignation. On Jesus she fixed all her affections; yet He is the victim whom she sacrificed, giving Him up to the most painful death the world ever wit-

My soul, behold thy Mother! Art thou not yet moved to compassion? Dost thou not sympathise with her? Ah! were I, indeed, a loving child of sorrow-stricken Mary, my heart would melt as ice before the flame—" my eyes would send forth springs of water," and I should "mourn as one mourneth for an only son."

When I see those whom I love in distress, I feel distressed myself; their sorrow afflicts me as though it were my own, and every sigh which escapes their breasts sinks into mine. Ah! then, let me show my love for Mary—let me take to heart her grief—and not only condole with her, but, by my life and conduct, endeavour to alleviate her sorrows.

But what was the act of this Dolorous Virgin when she revived after the first pangs of her anguish? She gently and meekly took from the arms of holy Simeon her darling babe, and, hastening to the Tabernacle, offered Him there, together with her own immaculate soul, to his Eternal Father.

There did she freely consent to all that had been foretold; then, with all the courage of the Queen of Martyrs, suffering in Him whom she loved far more than in herself, she literally fulfilled what was prefigured by the obedience of Abraham, when he prepared to sacrifice his son Isaac, and gave sentence with heroic firmness on her only child, saying—

"Eternal Father, since it is thy will that my Son should suffer and die—since my heart must be completely broken by pangs of grief, I am prepared for all, and humbly submit. Not my will, but thine be done."

"Mary knew how to accept, without complaint and without murmur, all that came from God; her pale lips were placed upon this chalice of wormwood and gall; she drained it even to the dregs, and then said sweetly, as she dried up her tears, 'O Lord, Thy will be done.'"[*] With all this fervour of her soul, she sacrificed Jesus.

---

[*] See Life of Blessed Virgin, by Orsini.

nessed! Oh, let me gain a lesson from her conformity to the Divine will in anguish and sorrow!

All, all of us have crosses to carry; all have trials to bear—trials from friends as well as from enemies—trials of body, trials of mind. As with Mary in the Temple, so with us, there are times when nothing is to be seen but blighted prospects and the shadows of some great impending sorrow. Some indeed, like her, have grief and tribulation for their daily portion; and no one can escape suffering at times. "Dispose of," says Thomas a Kempis, in his golden book of the Imitation of Christ, "and order all things as thou wilt and it may seem best to thee, thou wilt still find something to suffer, either willingly or unwillingly, and so thou wilt still find a cross."

Ah, let me then take courage from the example of my Blessed Mother! I will wipe away my tears and imitate her in holy resignation to the most wise designs of Providence. I will say with her to the Heavenly Father:

Heavenly Father! Thou art most wise in thy treatment of the sons of men. It is thy blessed will that this world should be to me a vale of tears. Here, like the Israelites in the desert, I taste the bitter waters of Mara, and spend my days in affliction and distress. Here, then, will I deny myself even what I might enjoy, and take up my cross after thy dear Son. Here will I follow my Jesus to Calvary; be it so. Do with me, O God, "not as I will, but as Thou wilt," afflict me as Thou pleasest. But permit me not to offend Thee again by sin. Thus wilt thou, my soul, like a true child of Mary, give honour and glory to the Most High, comfort the afflicted heart of thy sorrowful mother, and possess that inward peace which she enjoyed in the midst of her unutterable anguish, and which her Son promised "to men of good will."

PRAYER.

Behold me, dearest Mother, at thy feet. I admire thy profound humility in fulfilling the laws of purification and presentation, from both which thou wast exempt in virtue of thy Divine Maternity. I repent of my pride—I implore of thee humility. Sincerely, with heartfelt grief, I condole with thee in the sorrow which overwhelmed thy pure soul when thou didst hear from the lips of holy Simeon the future sufferings of thy Divine Son: I beseech thee, let me be a sharer in it. I admire and contemplate thy wonderful fortitude, and thy exemplary resignation, in the offering thou didst make of thy Saviour and thy Child. I humbly petition for the like resignation in all my trials and afflictions, and in the fulfilment of God's adorable will.

Mary, dolorous Mother! hear my prayers, and bless thy child, kneeling before thee. Amen.

Ejaculation.

Mother most sorrowful, obtain for me, from thy blessed Son, true humility and perfect resignation.

Say "three *Ave Marias*, in honour of all the sufferings of the Blessed Virgin in Bethlehem, for an increase of *Faith*."

ON THE SECOND DOLOUR OF MARY.

Mary's Flight into Egypt.

FIRST POINT.

No sooner was Jesus born than He began to be persecuted by Herod, who then ruled over the Jews. This ambitious prince, hearing that the long-expected Messias was come into the world "to deliver his people, Israel," was seized with envy and alarm. He feared lest this Saviour should supplant him in his authority and usurp his throne; therefore he sought to destroy him whilst he was yet a helpless babe. When the wise men came to Jerusalem from the east, enquiring "Where is He who is born King of the Jews?" Herod, thinking the time had arrived to rid himself of his supposed rival, called them privately, and learned diligently of them at what time the star which guided them from the East had first appeared: then, sending them into Bethlehem, he said: "Go, and diligently enquire after the child; and when you have found Him, bring me word again, that I also may come and adore Him." He hoped, by this deceitful stratagem, to obtain possession of our Lord. But, like all God's enemies, in the long run he deceived himself; for our Lord's "time was not yet come" to be betrayed and put to death.

After the wise men had found Jesus, adored him and presented before him their choicest gifts of gold, frankincense and myrrh, they were warned by a token from God that they should not return to Herod. They therefore went back another way into their own country.

When the envious tyrant found that his impious plans were thus brought to nought, like Pharao, King of Egypt, he hardened his heart yet further, and formed the cowardly and savage design of slaying by the sword every male child in that part of the country from two years old and under. For he concluded from what the Magi had told him, that the Messias would surely be among the victims to his cruelty. But it is the extreme of folly for man to oppose the Creator and fight against his God. Here, again, Herod's wicked purposes are most wonderfully brought to nothing. He hoped by thus murdering all the male infants in and about Bethlehem, that Jesus would also be slain. But after the Magi had departed, an angel of the Lord appeared in sleep to Joseph, saying:

"Arise, and take the child and his mother, and fly into Egypt, and be there until I shall tell thee; for it will come to pass that Herod will seek the child to destroy Him."

And here let me contemplate the cause of Mary's second Dolour.

St. Joseph, obedient to the command of the Heavenly messenger, at once arose and hastened to the Blessed Virgin, telling her what had been made known to him. Then, indeed, it was that the second sword transfixed the heart of Mary. How bitter, exclaims St. John Chrysostom, must have been the pain which was excited in the heart of Mary when she heard of the exile of herself and Son! "And, indeed," says St. Alphonsus, "what greater tribulation could there be, than that a poor young mother should be forced to fly with her new-born babe far away from home, from friends to strangers, from the hallowed sanctuary of the Lord to the polluted temples of devils." It was at the dead of night that the Blessed Virgin heard from the lips of St. Joseph the afflicting news; and, to add to her grief and embarrassment, the journey to Egypt was very long and toilsome, nor had she the provisions to sustain them on it. Mary doubtless reflected upon all these difficulties; great indeed, therefore, must have been her distress. She feared for the safety of her Child—she trembled for her spouse—she trembled for herself; nevertheless, she was perfectly obedient to the voice of Heaven. Nor did she complain of her lot; but, seated upon an ass, with Jesus in her arms and Joseph by her side, she departed at once from Bethlehem.

Mary knew perfectly that the fruit of her womb was God. She knew that although his Divine Majesty had humbly clothed Himself with human nature, He had not therefore lost the attributes of the Deity. Hence she was well aware that He still held in his Omnipotent hand the slender thread of Herod's life, and that, did Jesus but will it, that impious tyrant would be deprived of throne and power and breath. She was not ignorant that, when "the earth was void and empty and darkness was upon the face of the deep," then by his Almighty word light was made, and "all things were created by Him and in Him"—moreover that, as the Apostle goes on to say, "by Him all things consist, and by his frown all would be destroyed." The same Omnipotence, she knew well, could laugh to scorn the kings of the earth, and that, should the sacred Humanity of her Child demand aid from the Eternal Father, He would give Him presently more than twelve legions of angels to sweep his enemies from the earth.

Therefore, when Joseph announced to her that they were to hasten with the Babe into Egypt in order to save his life, we may imagine her speaking such words as these: Why need we fear Herod's wildest attempts? Why fly from a power that cannot touch or harm us? What can man do against my Son? Is He not truly God? Moreover, has not his enemy been already twice defeated in his plans? Why not this time also? Let us then remain here in peace and confidence. But does the Blessed Virgin thus excuse herself from the toils and pains which the Heavenly message enjoined? Far from it! She knew that the Divine will is ever to be obeyed; she knew also that such was the desire of her Divine Child. Hence, on hearing from Joseph the message of the Archangel, she at once complied, and, without the delay of a moment, the Holy

Family set out on their long journey of obedience—certain of the command, uncertain of its duration. This only did they know, that they were to remain in Egypt until the Archangel spoke again.

Let me here contemplate the prompt obedience of the Mother of God—how it puts to shame my past obstinacy and self-will.

Ten great commandments has my Creator given me. Do I fulfil them? Do I sincerely worship Him by faith, hope and charity? If not, my obedience is most unlike that of Mary. Do I ever take the name of the Lord, my God, in vain? If so, I am disobedient. Do I observe devoutly the Sabbath day? If not, I am not like Mary. Am I truly obedient to my parents, to my pastors, and other lawful superiors? If not, I am far indeed from being like Mary. Do I from time to time foolishly allow anger on my brow? Do I ill-treat my neighbour or ever seek revenge? Am I given to a life of debauchery, or to the sins of uncleanness? Do I wrong any one in his property by negligence, stealth, or fraud? Have I at any time robbed another person of his good name, or tarnished his character by unnecessary or lying informations? Have I ever desired my neighbour's wife, or envied his acquirements or his riches? Oh, if I have not kept the holy precepts which God has given me, surely I can claim no resemblance to her who, in obedience to the will of Heaven — despite the greatest inconvenience of time, of distance and fatigue—forsook her dearest friends, her much-loved home, to live in exile in an unknown land. Pray, then, my soul—pray fervently to this Holy Virgin, and cease not until she grants thy supplication, and obtains for thee from her Son the virtue of heroic obedience. Thus wilt thou be enabled to overcome all thy enemies; for, as Solomon testifies, "The obedient man shall speak of victory."

SECOND POINT.

Let me accompany this afflicted

Mother into Egypt, and compassionate her on the long and cheerless journey thither. The distance from Bethlehem to Heliopolis, the city in which the Holy Family took refuge, was very great, and appears still greater when we consider the imperfect modes of conveyance then in use. It is commonly said to have been about four hundred miles, and was rarely accomplished in less than forty days. The way was rough, unfrequented, and wild; the season the very depth of winter. Neither hospitable house nor warm clothing defended from its severity this tender Virgin and her still more tender Child. No doubt she had frequently to contend with violent storms and winds, and vainly endeavoured to shield her infant from the snow or rain. Great indeed must have been her sufferings! I seem to see her from time to time fainting from sheer fatigue. Had she been as robust as other women, the severity of this journey might not have weakened her so greatly; but tradition tells us that she was of a most delicate frame; moreover, she was then very young, being no more than fifteen or sixteen years of age, and had but just become a mother. What added yet more to her sorrow was that no food remained either for St. Joseph or herself. The little provision which in their haste they had brought with them, must have been soon consumed, and perhaps for half the journey none could be procured. During that long and toilsome way, Mary had also to give nourishment to her Son. Alas! poor Mother! how must his piteous cries have pierced her heart! "What greater pang," says St. Alphonsus, "can a mother suffer than to behold her child weak and hungry, and be unable to minister to its wants?"

Nor were these the only sufferings endured by the Blessed Virgin during the flight into Egypt. Those who travel now, even the poorest, can get some lodging, however humble, where they can rest at night and find a shelter from the wind and rain. But it was not so with the Mother of God. She was for nearly forty days exposed to the severities of the winter, with only the bare ground to sleep upon, and with no roof to shield her from the storm.

Oh! how can I pamper my body when I contemplate the Mother of the Most High vainly endeavouring each night to rest her wearied frame on the damp earth; in vain! for how could she possibly close her eyes in sleep, when she feared each moment lest some wild beast, or, still more terrible, some messenger from Herod might come to rob her of her child! Half of her perilous journey was through thick forests, half through the wilderness of Arabia. Whilst in the former, the falling of withered leaves, the rustling of shrubs, and the crackling of the branches of trees, sounded, most likely, to her attentive ear, like unto the near approach of robbers or the coming of ravenous wolves. When in the latter, she had to traverse over long tracts of sand, with no shelter whatever, and exposed completely to thirst, dust, excessive heat or excessive cold, according to the state of weather on each successive day. No doubt the drifting of the sands, the darkening of the sky, and the thick mists of noon and morning, must have alarmed her greatly lest some fierce hurricane might break out and destroy them in the wilderness.

But, oh! how far more must she have feared lest, on account of all these severities of the journey, she might lose her life's sole happiness, her darling Babe, lest He might die; "for Mary," says St. Bonaventure, "was not so much concerned for her own sufferings as for those of Jesus." She would keep her dear Son from danger of dew and cold, but how could she? She presses Him to her loving breast; but all in vain, for she herself is totally unprovided for the inclemencies of the weather. Had she the means, she would also comfort St. Joseph; but what help could she give him? She could administer nothing to him save encouraging words, and this no doubt she did, in spite of fatigue of body and of mental anguish. Hagar, in the desert of Beersheba, is a striking picture of the Blessed Virgin in her flight into Egypt. The Sacred Scripture tells us, in the 21st chapter of Genesis, that the water being exhausted, Hagar placed her son, Ismael, under a tree, and, withdrawing from him that she might not see him die, she abandoned herself to tears and groans until the angel came to console her. But Thou, O God, alone knowest how greatly Mary was convulsed with grief when she beheld the sufferings of her Child. I ask for grace to understand this great affliction, which even angels cannot comprehend without special light from Thee. Let this sorrow of thy daughter, O Heavenly Father, be deeply imprinted on my heart, that I may lovingly compassionate her who suffered with so much patience! This much, however, is granted me to know, that her affliction for her Divine Son must have almost infinitely surpassed in pain all the tears, groans, despair, and anguish of broken-hearted Hagar: since Mary fully understood that the life of Jesus was far more precious than the lives of all the children of Adam.

From the mournful journey of Mary with her spouse and child, through dark and wild woods, and through the Arabian desert, Christians are to learn, says Cornelius a Lapide, how to deport themselves during their long pilgrimage in this vale of tears. The world is the road to Heaven. But it is a very rough and dangerous path; experience teaches this to all. As I travel onwards, I am blown to and fro by contrary winds of temptation, while the rain of persecution and tribulation beats hard against me, or reproach, like snow, freezes my heart. Since such is indeed the case, I must never forget the afflicted Mother of God. She is patient under all her fatigues and sufferings. I must also be patient. She does not care for the severities of the season, nor should I be cast down by afflictions; I should courageously combat against them, asking the help of God's grace. She delays not on her journey, but makes it with great speed; neither should I, therefore, suffer the foolish toys of this world to stop my progress towards Heaven.

Oh! my soul, when, during thy exile here below, thou seemest rather to be struggling amidst tempests and whirlwinds than living in serenity, forget not Mary on her way to Egypt, if thou wouldst not be destroyed by the storms. If the strong winds of temptation blow, be not afraid, but look at Mary in the desert. If from time to time thou art beaten on all sides by the violent rain of pride, ambition, detraction, or jealousy, consider Mary in the desert. If the terrible thunders or the ravaging lightnings of anger, hatred, or revenge, disturb thy peace; or if despair, like a blight, withers the heart, think of the conduct of thy Mother in the woods and desert; see her patience, her faith, her unbounded hope, her entire reliance on the providence of God. If, my soul, the dust of imperfection or the gloom of the journey trouble or discourage thee, remember Mary on her way to Egypt. If the filth and mire of lust impede thee on thy way, do not forget Mary. In dangers, in anguish, anxiety, and doubt—in all thy troubles during thy pilgrimage towards Heaven, think of Mary in the desert. Let her sorrow there never depart from thy mind, thy heart, thy lips. Following her, thou wilt not go astray; praying to her, thou wilt not despair; led by her hand, thou wilt not fall to the ground; under her protection, thou needest not fear; she being leader, thou wilt not be fatigued; and by her gentle guidance thou wilt happily reach thy destination, where, with the holy angels, thou wilt praise her forever. (See St. Bernard, on the Name of Mary.)

PRAYER.

Behold, most afflicted Mother, thy humble client praying at thy feet. Here will I kneel, contemplating thy wonderful obedience and heroic patience: thy wonderful obedience in fulfilling so readily the onerous command of Gabriel, the Archangel; thy heroic patience in doing so without murmur or complaint. O Mary, dearest Virgin Mary, obtain for me, I beseech thee, these two beautiful virtues. Teach me also how to journey safely through this vale of tears. Comfort me in my sorrows, help me in my wants, and never suffer me to deviate from the right path, but as a star guides the mariner securely into port, so do thou, my protectress, conduct me safely to Heaven. Most sincerely do I compassionate thee in that indescribable woe which thou didst feel when in the dreary desert, and I devoutly beg of thee to stamp deeply on my heart thy second bitter Dolour, that with thee, dear afflicted Mother, I may suffer and weep here below, and be glad and rejoice with thee in Heaven. Amen.

Ejaculation.

Mary, O Dolorous Virgin, obtain for me holy patience and obedience, and safely conduct me through the perils of this world to Jesus, the haven of salvation.

Say "three *Ave Marias* in honour of all Mary suffered in Nazareth, for an increase of *Hope.*"

ON THE THIRD DOLOUR OF MARY.

Mary loses Jesus for Three Days.

FIRST POINT.

It has been said by many learned and pious writers that the third Dolour of the Blessed Virgin surpassed in intensity all her preceding sorrows; and no doubt they had great reasons for maintaining such an opinion. For, in her other Dolours Mary was not deprived of the sight, company, and heavenly conversation of her Divine Son; whereas in this she was entirely separated from Him, and at the same time she was perfectly ignorant of the cause of his absence, as well as the place of his stay. The heartrending pain which our Blessed Lady felt on occasion of this third Dolour, will be the subject of this meditation.

The Jews were wont three times in the year to go from all parts of Israel to visit at Jerusalem the Temple of the Lord. There they offered their gifts of doves, pigeons, goats, lambs, and oxen. There they presented to the God of Abraham, Isaac, Jacob, and Moses, their homage of love, praise, adoration, and thanksgiving. There they joyously and piously sang hymns and celebrated their solemn feasts. The chief of these solemnities, which the Levitical Law ordered to be strictly observed, was the Paschal Festival or Passover—a feast to commemorate the happy deliverance of Jacob's posterity from the hands of Pharao and from the Egyptian slavery. Now, St. Joseph was accustomed every year to go to the Temple at the appointed times. When, therefore, our dear Lord was about twelve years of age, it being the Pasch, this holy man went as usual to Jerusalem, accompanied by Jesus and his Mother. When they arrived at the place of their destination, it is commonly believed that they separated, and that each one joined a different party. St. Joseph went with the men; Mary joined the women, and our Saviour accompanied his Mother. Neither Jesus nor Mary was bound on this occasion to visit the Temple. The law obliged only men to go; still our Blessed Lady went, as well as St. Joseph, devoutly to celebrate the Paschal solemnity. Why then does she visit the Temple? and why does she take her beloved Son? The learned Cornelius a Lapide answers, that "Mary accompanied her saintly spouse to Jerusalem, and went to the Tabernacle of the Lord through devotion, but that she took Jesus with her in order to teach mothers how very careful they ought to be to make their children, whilst still young, eagerly seek the Temple and affectionately love the God who therein resides." St. Alphonsus and Venerable Bede make the same comment. Alas! how extremely negligent mothers are in this very important duty. As soon as their children are able to run about, they are suffered to wander from home without necessity, to amuse themselves in public streets, to play in bye-ways and roads, in a word, to do just as their whims suggest. It is not uncommon now-a-days to hear children call each other fool—deride their parents and use against them opprobrious epithets—to hear them declare most positively that they will not do what they are told. And whose fault is it? It is assuredly the mother's. It is her duty to watch over her children, to keep them from bad company and from the occasion of sin. She is strictly bound to teach them their prayers, to send them to school early, to take them to church, and to instil into their tender hearts great love for God and his sacred worship. But if she neglect these duties, her children will be to her a scourge; they will be a reproach. When they grow up they will shorten her days, and, perhaps, God knows! perhaps they will be the occasion of her eternal ruin. This, however, is certain, that the mother will have to answer at the dread tribunal of the Lord, for the misdeeds of her neglected offspring, and woe to her if she has unhappily forgotten her duty in their regard. Woe to her if she has thoughtlessly suffered them to play indiscriminately with other children, woe to her if she has not deeply imprinted on their minds great love for God, and an especial esteem for his house! For, if she has thus been negful of the fruit of her womb, the Omnipotent Judge will condemn her as one highly culpable, as a cruel tyrant to her children; yea, and which is still more deplorable, He will punish her as their murderer and as the cause of their eternal condemnation. Oh! if you be a parent, who now read these lines, earnestly attend to this admonition: it is of most vital importance; it is the voice of the Lord speaking to your heart. "Harden not your hearts, but listen awfully to the words of God your Saviour." Imitate the example of the Blessed Virgin; she, like a prudent and virtuous parent, took to the Temple whilst very young her Divine Son Jesus; she did so, as you have seen, for your particular instruction. Profit, therefore, by so useful a lesson, and resolve to be more vigilant over your offspring, and bring them up in the love and fear of their Creator. If you do this your family will be your joy, your honour, your crown. Your sons and daughters will grow up round you, like stately cedars of Libanus. They will condole with you in your sorrows; they will minister to your wants; they will assist you in sickness and infirmity; and will be your staff and delight in old age and your companions in Heaven. "A wise son maketh his father joyful."

Beg pardon, therefore, now for your past want of care, and daily beseech Mary to teach you to educate your children properly and to preserve them from all evil. Finally, never forget the inspired words of David, the Royal Psalmist, which may be more especially applied to the young. "With the holy thou wilt be holy; and with the innocent thou wilt be innocent; and with the alert thou wilt be alert; and with the perverse thou wilt be perverted." If you bear this truth always in mind, and keep the example of Mary always before your eyes, there will be no danger of your neglecting the welfare of your family; but as a good parent you will strive to the best of your power not only to save your own soul, but you will endeavour to save the souls of your dear children, too, that so you may have the unspeakable happiness of reigning eternally with them in Paradise.

SECOND POINT.

After the solemn celebration of the Pasch, Joseph and Mary returned home, each by a different route, and with a different party. But Jesus, alas! remained behind. When they arrived at the place at which they were to meet, the distance of a day's journey from the Temple, this holy couple were greatly alarmed to find that Jesus had been left at Jerusalem, for each one expected to see Him in the company of the other. "And when Jesus was twelve years old, they going up into Jerusalem according to the custom of the feast," says St. Luke, "and having fulfilled the days, when they returned, the child Jesus remained in Jerusalem, and his parents knew it not." Judge, then, my soul, how exceedingly great must have been the grief of Mary when she discovered herself for the first time to be deprived of her most beloved Son. He was her heart's delight, her peace, her joy, her happiness, her all. His voice was to her ears the sweetest and the most melodious music. His divine kisses like honey to her virgin lips; his company was heaven here below. Without Him this world was blank; without Him life was wretchedness indeed—yea, death, for she cared for nought else besides Him. Methinks that now I hear this afflicted Mother, when first she meets her husband, address him thus: "Where is my Jesus?" To which earnest inquiry St. Joseph replies, "I do not know; I thought that He had returned with you." "No, no," cries Mary, "He has not, He is not here. I have not seen Him; I expected to find Him with you; alas! alas! He is

of having offended Him. When a fond mother loses her child she is disconsolate; she sighs, she mourns, she groans, she weeps, nor can she sleep until she finds him. Now, Mary was the fondest of mothers; all her love, too, was centred upon an only Son, and He was Divine; He was truly God. Judge, then, my soul, of the severity of her woe. Hence St. Laurence Justinian says, "there never was a greater grief than Mary's, because there never was a child more loved than Jesus." Is it possible for her at night to repose in peace, when she has not yet found her Son? After enquiring at every house, after going from street to street in search of her lost treasure, Mary returns to her lodgings, and finds herself for the first time a childless Mother. Oh! what a sad and weary night does Mary pass: in vain does she attempt to close her eyes: she cannot sleep. As soon as day breaks and the sun once more appears, this dolorous Mother is seen again in search of Jesus; but this day also she meets with no success, and sorrowfully returns home for the second time without her Son. Once more, therefore, does she pass the night in bitterness and weeping. Again the morning comes; again she seeks our Lord. The women of Jerusalem compassionate her; but they cannot comfort her, because they have not found her child. Like Rachel, Mary bewailed and sorely lamented, and, like her, she was not to be comforted, because she had lost the fruit of her womb. Wherefore, in the Office of the Seven Dolours, Holy Church places on her lips the lamentation of the prophet Isaias over Juda, which we find in the 22nd chapter of the Prophecy of Isaias, "Therefore I have said, depart from me, I will weep bitterly: labour not to comfort me."

For three days and three nights the Blessed Virgin was a childless Mother, and it was not until the third day that she found Him whom she had lost. On this day, after much anxiety and seeking, after labour and fatigue, after praying and weeping, having gone to

Jerusalem, to her unspeakable surprise and delight she discovered Jesus in the Temple sitting in the midst of the doctors and elders, disputing with them and instructing them concerning the Messias. "I found Him whom my soul loveth, I held Him and will not let Him go."

St. Alphonsus says that this Dolour of Mary should console all who find themselves in desolation and are bereft of that comfort which once they experienced in the presence of the Lord. God is wont from time to time to chastise those whom He loves. He frequently hides Himself and leaves the soul in spiritual dryness and desolation. When they are only children in virtue, before they are fully initiated in perfection, He is accustomed to feed them with milk and honey, and from time to time He gives them a foretaste of that celestial nectar promised the blessed; but when they have grown robust and strong, as with the Apostles after the descent of the Holy Ghost, He wisely distributes the wholesome bread of tribulation. Oh! then, my soul, when thou art thus deprived of the sensible presence of thy Saviour, when thou art in a state of spiritual dryness and affliction of spirit, thou shouldst meditate on what Mary suffered when she had lost her beloved Son; and thou shouldst learn from her example to control thy alarm when thou art unconscious of sin. For though, during the three days' absence of Jesus, each moment seemed an eternity to her most loving heart, still she never lost confidence in God. Be encouraged, therefore, my soul, and do not yield to despondency because now and then Divine Providence wishes to prove and purify thee in the sacred crucible of humiliation.

But what if thou hast lost Jesus through thy own fault? Then, indeed, there are great reasons why thou shouldst seek Him sorrowing. By losing Jesus thou losest thy sovereign good, and thus deprivest thyself of the everlasting enjoyment of infinite beauty, wisdom, love, power, and felicity, and all the other infinite attributes which spring from the Divine Essence. By losing Jesus, thou dost completely forfeit all claim to the kingdom of Heaven, purchased by his Precious Blood. By losing Jesus, thou dost lose peace of mind and thy bodily health, and oftentimes thou art in danger of losing thy life. And lastly, thou dost also lose all liberty of spirit and dost become a prisoner of the devil—like him, condemned to the "everlasting pains of hell."

Oh! then, if thou shouldst ever be so unfortunate, my soul, as to fall into mortal sin and lose God's grace, seek Jesus sorrowing until thou dost find Him, as Mary did. She could neither eat, drink, nor sleep without her Son. Canst thou, then, close thy eyes at night when separated from thy Saviour? Canst thou live in peace and find happiness without Him? Oh! "what will it profit thee if thou shouldst gain the whole world and thereby lose thy immortal soul?" "For what can a man give in exchange for his soul?" "If, O Man," says St. Augustine, "thou hadst two souls, then, indeed, thou couldst afford to lose one, to give one to God and one to the devil, to destine one for Heaven and to condemn the other to hell; but since thou hast only one soul, thou shouldst rather lose all the world can give, than lose thy one precious soul." My soul, examine thyself. Art thou now in the grace of God, or hast thou lost thy God by sin? Oh! if the latter be thy sad condition, make haste, do not delay, begin at once, seek Him, and when once more thou shalt possess Him, never let Him depart from thee again.

PRAYER.

O Mary, dear Mother of Jesus, thy affectionate heart was broken with grief, when for the space of three days thou didst lose thy beloved Son; but thou didst not rest until thou hadst found Him. Do, then, I most humbly beseech thee, teach me how to find Jesus, if I am so unfortunate as to lose Him by sin. I, indeed, deserve to be deprived of his blessed company; thou didst not deserve such an affliction, yet thou didst seek Him sorrowing. Oh! then obtain for me that I, too, may seek my Saviour with tears and lamentation. Thou, O Mary, couldst not repose in sleep without first finding Jesus; may I never, therefore, lie down to rest separated from my God by sin. Hear, oh hear my prayer! Despise not my humble supplication, and if it so happen that Heaven would try me by desolation and affliction, teach me, O Dolorous Virgin, how to deport myself, how to carry my cross with joy and peace; and be thou thyself my joy and consolation. When thou didst go to the Temple thou didst take Jesus with thee; teach, therefore, parents how to bring up their children in the love and fear of God; in respect for Holy Church and sacred worship. This, dear Mother, is all I ask. Hear and bless me, for I am thy client and thy Son's adopted child. Amen.

Ejaculation.

Thou who didst seek thy lost Son

for three days, obtain for me by thy cruel sorrow, never to be torn from Him by sin, and by grace soon to find Him if I have lost Him.

Say "three *Ave Marias* in honour of all the Blessed Virgin suffered in the Deserts of Arabia, for an increase of *Divine Love.*"

ON THE FOURTH DOLOUR OF MARY.

Mary meets her Divine Son bearing his Cross to Calvary.

FIRST POINT.

When sentence of death had been passed, by unjust Pontius Pilate, upon Jesus Christ, St. John, together with several other Apostles, hastened to make known to Mary the lamentable tidings. From the lips of these she learned the time of her Son's execution. They told her where it was to take place, and the road along which He was to carry the cross. As soon as the Blessed Virgin heard this sad intelligence, she hastened to meet her suffering Jesus. Here began her fourth Dolour, for on this occasion her immaculate heart was for the fourth time transfixed with a sword of grief. Contemplate, my soul, this dire sorrow, and compassionate her who endured it; for no other of God's creatures ever merited compassion as much as Mary.

The Blessed Virgin had not proceeded far before Jesus met her view. Was it her Son whom in the distance she descried? Alas! how changed! Once He was the fairest among the sons of men, the most perfect, the most beautiful. The Divinity shone in his very countenance; grace and majesty accompanied his every step, and angels loved to gaze upon Him. But now, care-worn and bruised, his sacred face defiled, his garments bathed in blood, his steps feeble and uncertain: bearing on his head a crown of thorns, and on his shoulders a heavy cross—oh! Mary, can this outcast be thy Son? Surely this is not Jesus, this cannot be God made Man. Yes, alas! yes, 'tis He; nor was it long ere Mary recognised Him. For, as she approached this Man of Sorrows, He fixed on her his eyes, from which He had removed the blood, and gave her one of those loving God-like glances, which when a babe He was wont to give when reclining his sacred head upon her Virgin bosom. No sooner does she recognize her Son than regardless of every obstacle, she flies to his embrace. But, oh God! what does she behold? His adorable mouth is perfectly saturated with blood, his beard and hair are torn and clotted with gore. With blood are his garments stained; with blood is his once lovely countenance horridly besmeared. Blood starts and falls, drop by drop, from his wounded face, blood trickles fast from his sacred temples and dyes the ground upon which He stands.

In this state Mary beholds her Divine Son. Oh! what an afflicting sight for so affectionate a Mother. Yea, a sight calculated to wring compassion from the heart of the most bitter foe. You who read this meditation, what would your feelings be, and what your language, were you to meet a child you love most dearly in such a state? Could you bear such a scene of woe? How could you? Your tears would flow in torrents, and, overwhelmed by grief, you would fall fainting at the feet of your suffering child.

If you would act thus, what must have been the shock which such a sight as I have pictured caused to Mary? Behold her bathed in tears, unable to restrain her grief; she utters piercing groans, she faints, she almost dies with anguish. Look down, O Blessed Spirits, from your thrones on high, and see your Queen prostrate upon the earth in agony, pierced by a sorrow greater than all the woes of every other creature.

As soon as the Blessed Virgin recovers from her death-like swoon, the same sad spectacle once more meets her view and fills her with dismay. But, careless of her grief, the cruel soldiers seize her slender wrists, drag her from the feet of her Divine Son, and rudely push her behind the mob. She cannot bear to be separated from her child's embrace; her grief, therefore, is increased a hundredfold. Oh! my soul, no imagination can conceive, no eloquence describe the depth, the bitterness, the poignancy of Mary's woe; it was far deeper than the ocean, and far more bitter than any kind of myrrh. We may with good reason imagine on the lips of the Blessed Virgin the Lamentation of Jeremias, "My soul is far removed from good things; for He hath filled me with bitterness, He hath inebriated me with wormwood." But in order to form a more vivid representation of the intensity of her sorrow, I must listen to St. Bernard. He says that all the affliction of the Blessed Virgin springs from her compassion for Jesus, and explains that in these words: "There are three things required on the part of the person that compassionates, relatively to the person that is compassionated. First, vehemence of pain; second, knowledge of that vehemence by the sympathiser; and thirdly, true friendship. The first, I say, is vehemence of pain. The bitterness of the sufferings of Christ cannot be told by tongues of men or angels, as they are beyond the capacity of any creature to understand. With regard to the second requisite, Mary had a very clear knowledge of our Saviour's pains, because the Mother stood by her Son even to his last moments, and was well aware that He was also the Son of God. Lastly, her love for Jesus was exceedingly great. She felt, therefore, almost infinite compassion during his Passion. But she would not have felt so much compassion had she not been witness of all his torments." Thus this great Doctor of the Church argues the intensity of Mary's woes. "To conceive," says Cornelius a Lapide, "the intensity of the sorrows of the Blessed Virgin, it would be necessary to know the ardour of her love for Jesus. But who can fathom this? In the immaculate heart of Mary there were two loves; the one supernatural, wherewith she loved Jesus as her God, the other natural, which excited her to love Him as her son. These two loves in Mary's soul formed one, but that a love so intense that the Blessed Virgin loved Jesus to such a degree, that a pure creature could not love Him more." Hence, as there was no love

F

like her love, so there was no grief like her grief, and as the love which she entertained for Jesus was almost infinite, so, too, must the pain which she felt in seeing Him in so pitiable a state have almost approached infinitude. Justly, then, does the Mother of God deserve to be styled by the Church the Queen of Martyrs; for she suffered more, in meeting her Son on his way to Calvary, than all those holy souls endured either by fire, or on the rack, in scalding oil, or freezing water, by cruel scourging, or by the sword. Oh, my soul, compassionate again this Dolorous Virgin, and if thou hast no tears to shed with her, at least learn of her to compassionate Jesus, "the Man of Sorrows."

When thou dost contemplate his sufferings and agony, when thou dost consider Him covered with wounds and blood, when thou dost meditate on his being scourged at the pillar in Pilate's Hall, crowned with thorns, bearing his cross, thrice falling under its weight, fastened to it by sharp nails, and agonizing and convulsed in death upon Mount Calvary, canst thou remain unmoved? If so, be assured, my soul, that thou hast little love for Jesus; for were thy love sincere, his anguish would be thy anguish, his pain thine; what tortured his flesh would torture thy heart, and like Mary, thou wouldst mourn over the afflictions of thy beloved. Oh learn then of the suffering Mother of God— learn to love Jesus thy Saviour; thus only wilt thou know how to compassionate Him in his Passion. For this purpose, say every day this short but salutary prayer: "Mary, Queen of Martyrs, teach me to love thy sweet Son Jesus, and to condole with Him in his crucifixion and death." And determine as long as thou livest never to forget the pains of her maternal heart, when she met her Child, like another Isaac, bearing on his shoulders the very wood on which He was to die.

SECOND POINT.

When the Blessed Virgin found

herself removed to a distance from her Son, she did not return from this most afflicting scene; but with heroic fortitude she patiently though sorrowfully followed him to Calvary. Jesus marks his footsteps with his blood; Mary traces out hers with tears of sorrow. He is bathed in gore, she is plunged in an ocean of grief; and as she follows our Lord in that sad procession, she is witness of all his afflictions; she hears the curses and blasphemies uttered by the brutal executioners; none of their insults and outrages escape her. She beholds the excitement of the rabble; they strike her innocent Son with heavy staves and with their hands. She sees some of these frantic wretches drag Him forward with a rope, and others push Him on behind; she witnesses the jeering, the laughter, the reproach of the infuriated mob. The rabble, like men possessed by evil spirits, run from place to place—now before her Son, now after Him; now they strike Him in the face, now they threaten Him and uplift their clenched hands, and now they cast large stones against Him. At one time they call Him a seducer of the people, then they declare Him to be a disturber of the public peace, a false prophet, and a blasphemer. Children point at Him with their fingers and revile Him as a fool. In a word, Mary beheld the soldiers and the populace vieing with each other, which could heap upon Jesus the greatest ignominy or cause Him the acutest pain. Surely this scene of cruelty and sin was sufficient to have occasioned her death. And it would have done so, says St. Anselm, had not God preserved her life by a singular miracle; and St. Bernard declares "that her sorrow was so exceedingly great, that were it divided among all men, it would suffice to cause them instant death." But Mary's grief ends not here ; for she sees her best Beloved fall under the heavy cross. She runs, no doubt, to his assistance, but she is rudely repulsed. Then at a little distance she views and contemplates his wounds and pains, and hears his sighs, and from the contracted features of his face she knows that He can scarcely breathe. O God! how does this Virgin's heart bleed!! and yet she cannot assist her Son! Oh that she could relieve Him of that burden! Oh that at least she could lift Him from the ground! But vain are her desires; she is not allowed. Now she hears the wicked soldiers gruffly command Him speedily to arise. "Get up," they yell, "or we will kill thee." And because He could not do as they would have Him, they push Him, they drag Him and beat Him as a slave. Of the Mother of the Machabees, who witnessed the tortures of her seven sons, St. Augustine remarks, that "what they suffered in their bodies she likewise endured in her soul; because she saw them tortured." The same happened to Mary the Mother of Jesus. The kicks—the blows—the cross—the falls which afflicted his tender body, entered her maternal heart and made her suffer. Yes, the scars and wounds scattered over his sacred flesh were imprinted on her compassionate heart. In the revelations of St. Agnes we read that the Blessed Virgin received as many strokes of the sword, through compassion, as she saw wounds in her crucified Son. Hence St. Laurence Justinian writes that the heart of the Blessed Virgin was a mirror of the sorrows of her Son, in which were fixedly represented the spittle, the buffets, the wounds, and all the torments of Jesus. What our dear Lord suffered in his body, she suffered in her soul, and the grief which was written on his countenance was deeply stamped on her loving heart. Three times does He fall under the cross on his way to Calvary; imagine therefore, my soul, her excessive grief.

But that which greatly increased Mary's sorrow, was the fact, that on none of these occasions was she permitted to comfort Him. She would, no doubt, were she allowed, have wiped the clotted blood from off his sacred face; she would have poured oil into his wounds, have presented water to his parched lips, and bathed with aromatics his burning brow; but the hard-hearted soldiers kept her far away from Him. O Mary, thou most afflicted of Mothers, how I feel and grieve for thee—would that I could comfort thee in thy sorrow! would that I could heal the wounds of thy bleeding Son! Ah! how willingly would I do so; but what can I a wicked sinner do? O my soul, if thou wouldst comfort Mary in her excessive woe, and stop the flowing blood of her Divine Son; if thou wouldst give her joy, help Him on his way to Calvary and lighten the burden which for thee He carries; follow Jesus to the place of crucifixion; in other words, deny thyself, take up thy cross and walk after Him. Yea! go along that path which, with his Precious Blood, He has traced out for thee. Ah! yes, this indeed is the grand lesson taught me by Mary on this occasion. If, therefore, I would relieve her pain and dry away her tears, I must for ever bid farewell to the vain joys, the unlawful pleasures, the dangerous pastimes of the world of sin, I must faithfully fulfil my baptismal vows: to speak more plainly, I must renounce the world with all its pomps, my flesh with all its delights, the devil with all his works, and "fly sin," as also the occasions thereof, as I would fly "from the face of a serpent." Yes, I must deny myself; I must generously and bravely take up my cross and courageously follow my crucified Saviour to the place where He was slain. This my Mother Mary has done; joyfully, therefore, will I study this salutary lesson taught by the Blessed Mother of God; joyfully will I take up my cross, joyfully will I carry it to the Mount of Sorrows; for thus and only thus can I give Mary pleasure, and solace her in her afflictions. This, therefore, is the resolution I make; yes, before Heaven I purpose to follow Mary in the footsteps of her bleeding Son.

Farewell, then, ye false and cheating pleasures, ye fleeting joys, ye vain amusements of this deceitful world;

farewell for ever. No more will I seek in you to indulge the cravings of my own ever hungry appetite; no more through you will I sin against my conscience and my God. Cheerfully now do I receive the Cross of Christ: I embrace it; I press it fervently to my heart and lips, and willingly shall I go with Mary to Calvary, to station myself beneath the tree of life, and to die with Jesus, as He died for me. Such were the noble sentiments of St. Andrew the Apostle, when the executioner led him to be crucified; and such shall be mine even to my last breath.

PRAYER.

O Mary, Queen of Martyrs! I grieve and mourn with thee. How great must have been thy pangs of grief and thy lamentations when thou didst meet thy beloved Son, crowned with thorns, loaded with a cross, and bathed in blood. Oh that I could fathom the depth and measure the breadth of thine affliction. But, since that is impossible, at least let me feel a part—yes, dear Mother, let me have a share in thy sorrows. I by my sins have caused all thy pain; therefore I, and I alone, deserve it all. Two most excellent lessons, on this occasion, thou hast taught me; one of love for Jesus, the other, to renounce this world and sin and to follow thy Son to Calvary. Obtain, therefore, for me, grace to practise that which thou didst teach by thy example, that, suffering with thee whilst on earth, I may deserve to reign for ever with thee in Heaven, and may with the Holy Angels praise thee and Jesus, singing joyous hymns unceasingly. Amen.

Ejaculation.

Mary, most afflicted Mother, obtain for me grace for the sake of the love of Jesus, to deny myself, to take up my cross and follow Him to Calvary.

Say "three *Ave Marias*, in honour of all Mary suffered in Egypt, for an increase of *Fraternal Charity.*"

ON THE FIFTH DOLOUR OF MARY.

Mary beholds the Crucifixion of Jesus.

FIRST POINT.

Great indeed must have been the pain of the Mothers of the Holy Innocents, when they witnessed their dear children cut to pieces by the sword of the tyrant Herod. But all their affliction united, so as to form one most dire sorrow, would be as nothing when compared with the heartrending woe which overpowered Mary's soul when she beheld the crucifixion of her Son. It is called her fifth Dolour, being the fifth sword of grief which transfixed her stainless heart.

The Blessed Virgin met Jesus on his way to Calvary, and thither did she follow Him sorrowing. As soon as He arrived at the place destined for the execution, the Cross was lifted off his mangled shoulders and laid upon the ground. Then the soldiers came around Him, and with demon-like fury stripped Him of his garments, and as they took these from Him, tore open once more his sacred flesh, for his clothes had by this time adhered to the innumerable wounds He had received. Ah, truly the lamentation of Mary must have been excessive indeed, when she beheld those festered wounds of her Son thus once more made to bleed!!

When everything was ready for the crucifixion, the Jews gave Jesus some drink, for in those days it was the custom to fortify criminals with a refreshing beverage before their execution. But, oh God! what is this draught which the afflicted Mother sees given to her dying Son? St. Matthew answers by saying: "And they gave Him wine to drink mingled with gall." How indignant must she not have felt? Surely this insult alone was of itself sufficient to break her heart? After the soldiers had thus shamefully mocked their God, they violently threw Him upon the cross. Scarcely had He outstretched his hands and feet upon its infamous arms, when, like hungry tigers leaping upon their prey, they fell upon his hallowed body and commenced their work of blood. My soul, stand with Mary and view this woeful spectacle, that thou mayest know how much she suffered from the sight. Some of the soldiers kneel upon his arms, some on his legs to hold them down; some stretch out the palms of his anointed hands and keep them flat and open; others press down his feet; then the murderous executioner uplifts the heavy hammer, strikes the fatal blows, and drives the nails through the nerves, arteries, veins, and muscles of our dear Lord's most tender hands and feet. First, he thus fixes to the cross the right hand, then the left, and then he nails down the feet. Oh, what must Mary have thought and felt when she beheld this barbarous deed!!! when she heard the hammer fall and saw the crimson tide streaming afresh from the wounds of her Son, when the blood began once more to flow from his forehead, mouth, and ears, and to fall drop after drop even from his eyes! St. Bridget says in her Revelations, that "fainting she fell on the ground in spasms of pain." St. Bernard, St. Laurence Justinian, Dionysius, Maldonatus, and St. Augustine, teach the same thing. Yes! the convulsions of the agonizing Son became the spasms of the Mother. Witness now, my soul, the anguish of our Lady. Poor afflicted Mary! her Virgin heart is chilled within her. It is broken: the wounds of her bleeding Son are deeply engraven on its very core. "The Dolour of my Child was my Dolour," said she herself to a great servant of the Lord, "because his heart was my heart." Yea, her sorrow was so great, that only God could tell its bitterness. "Tongue cannot describe, nor can the intellect understand with what exceeding grief were the pious bowels of Mary moved," says her devoted client St. Bernard, when she was present at the Crucifixion of Jesus. O Mary, dear Mother, how I grieve to see thee in this pitiable state! What can I do to ease thy pain, to stop thy tears, to deliver thee from such oceans of sorrow? "To what shall I compare thee? or to what shall I liken thee, O daughter of Jerusalem? to what shall I equal thee that I may comfort thee, O Virgin daughter of Sion? for great as the sea is thy destruction: who shall heal thee?" Ah! methinks I hear this Dolorous Virgin say, in answer, some such words as these, in a most plaintive voice: "If thou wouldst comfort my afflicted heart, heal the wounds of my crucified Son. Thou hast caused them by sin; heal them now by repentance; for I cannot recover from my sorrow unless thou take away the cause."

Oh yes, my soul, if thou wouldst compassionate Mary, soothe her bleeding heart and dry away her tears, thou must wash the blood from the body of her Son, thou must pour oil into his wounds, thou must heal his hands and feet, by sincere repentance of thy wicked life. Thy sins have crucified the Lord, and only by contrition canst thou repair the evil thou hast done. Repent, therefore, repent without delay.

During the whole time of the crucifixion of her Son, Mary was most patient. She endured all her sufferings without murmuring, nor did she seek vengeance on those who afflicted Jesus. "Mary," says St. Anselm, "did not lacerate herself in the midst of so much bitterness; she did not desire evil to befall her enemies, nor did she murmur or seek from God revenge upon them; but she was most patient." Yes, the Blessed Virgin was most patient in her sorrows. Endeavour, my soul, to resemble her in the practice of this most necessary virtue. Patience is a virtue by which, with even temper, we endure the ills of this life, so that on their account we are not disturbed exteriorly, nor made sorrowful interiorly, so as to allow ourselves in anything to offend against the holy will of God. What is my behaviour? How do I deport myself in trouble? Am I silent when afflicted by God or injured by man? If not, I am not patient like Mary, who was silent when before her eyes her innocent Son was nailed to the Cross. When insulted by my neighbours, derided by enemies, or forsaken by friends, do I murmur or complain? If so, I am no imitator of Mary. If unwell, or suffering under any other tribulation, do I lament and mourn? If so, I am certainly far from being like Mary, who, although her grief was enough to have caused her death, was patient and resigned, free from reproof and angry murmuring. Oh, indeed, I must own that I am not patient; but, by the grace of God, and through thy intercession, O Mary, I shall soon become so. These are the acts of patience which I resolve daily to practise. In cold and heat, and in every other change of season, to be resigned; in pains and diseases of the body, in sadness and fatigue, in hunger and thirst, in poverty and want, never to complain; to bear patiently with the characters and inclinations of men, no matter how much opposed to my views; in ignominy and degradation, in loss of friends,—yea, in death itself, to be tranquil; in derision and insult, never to be angry. Finally, in anxiety of spirit, in desolation and dryness, in obscurities, in scruples and temptations, frequently to repeat the words of Holy Job: " As it has pleased the Lord, so it is done ; blessed be the name of the Lord."

SECOND POINT.

Whilst the Blessed Virgin had her weeping eyes fixed upon her bleeding Son, the executioners hoisted the cross into the air, and let it fall heavily into the hole prepared for it. As soon as this was done, Mary advanced to the foot of this bed of sorrow, and stationed herself beside her dying Child. "Now there stood by the cross his Mother," says St. John, and as she thus gazes upon her beloved Son, she attentively listens to his sighs, and counts his wounds. He once was beautiful, but now his whole body is distorted, his head is bowed down with distress and pain, his eyes are closed and sunken in his head, and his face is defiled with clotted blood and the disgusting spittle of his persecutors. Whilst thus she looks at Jesus, she hears the shouts and yells of the frantic mob, and her pure ears are shocked by blasphemies uttered against his adorable Divinity. "Vah, vah!" they cry, wagging their heads, "vah! Thou that destroyest the Temple of God, and in three days dost rebuild it, save thyself; if Thou be the Son of God, come down from the cross." In the midst of all these insults, Mary perceives that her Son pants hard for breath, and sighs deeply. At last she hears Him call for drink. "Sitio," says He, "I thirst," whereupon she witnesses the soldiers, with barbarity unheard of, press into his mouth a sponge steeped in vinegar. Oh, what dire sorrow for such a tender Mother. Mary may now, indeed, truly exclaim, "Oh, all you that pass by the way, attend and see if there be grief like unto my grief."

But in order to understand the agony of this afflicted Virgin's heart on this melancholy occasion, it is necessary to call to mind again the greatness of her love for Jesus. For our compassion for the miseries of others is proportioned to the affection we entertain towards them. So that, if we do not love them, we feel no compassion for them; if we love them but little, then in their troubles we only compassionate them a little; but, if we love them much, our sorrow, too, is great, when we see them suffer. Hence all the grief which afflicts the human heart is but as a drop of water to the ocean when compared to the unfathomable grief which the maternal heart of Mary endured at the foot of the cross; far deeper was it than the measureless sea! far more bitter than anything we can imagine. The reason, indeed, is obvious, because her love for her Son almost infinitely surpassed all human affection. For when had mother a more tender child, or one more lovely than Mary's best beloved Jesus, in whom she had more than all the world could bestow. The Blessed Virgin was dead to herself, she lived only in her Son's life. And when at last her loved one died, then did her soul seem torn from her, and as her love for Him was but one, and far above every other love, so this her sorrow was but one, and far above all other sorrows. His face had beamed forth rays of heavenly light. To think of Him had been the greatest happiness of her heart, to speak of Him was sweeter than the language of angels, to hear his words was music to her soul. He was the joy of her life, her only consolation. Heaven aud earth, indeed, and all that is in them, she possessed in Him. "His name was as oil poured out, and gave great nourishment to her mind, and was sweeter than honey to her virgin lips. She cared for nought but Jesus. So when she saw her love suspended upon the cross in mortal agony, what must she not have suffered? Oh, what a moment was that!

her heart trembled, and was convulsed in most intense agony. She looked up, but she could not help her child; she looked around her, but saw only those who had nailed Him to the cross; then she sighed aloud, and fell prostrate upon the ground. Oh, how little is the world to this afflicted Mother!! She has lost all strength, and yet with perfect self-control she raises her voice and speaks to Jesus, half complainingly: "Oh, my child, my child, to whom wilt thou leave thy wretched mother? Oh, who will permit me to die with thee? Cruel, cruel death, why sparest thou me? Take away the mother, leave her not childless; to her, life is more hard to be borne than death, bereft of Thee."*

Whilst thus the Queen of Martyrs lifted up her voice in heartrending lamentation, her crucified Jesus thus addressed her: "Woman, behold thy Son;" thus commending her to the custody of St. John, and leaving this

---

* See Henry Suso's little book on Eternal Wisdom.

disciple to comfort and take care of her; then having cried aloud to his Eternal Father, bowing down his head, He gave up the ghost." Ah! methinks I can see this Dolorous Mother overwhelmed with grief, sink once more speechless beneath the blood-stained cross. And when recovering from her death-like swoon, she casts from time to time a glance upon her lifeless Son, which renews each time her bitter grief. The rite of leprosy commanded in the 14th chapter of Leviticus, is now most painfully and literally fulfilled to wash away the sins of man. The rite of leprosy ordained that he who was to be purified should offer two sparrows, and that one of the sparrows should be immolated over living waters. "But the other that is alive, the priest shall dip in the blood of the sparrow that is immolated, wherewith he shall sprinkle him that is to be cleansed seven times; and he shall let go the living sparrow that it may fly into the field." The sparrow immolated is a figure of Jesus crucified, dead on the altar of the cross.

But the sparrow dipped in the blood of the dead one, and let fly into the fields, represents the most afflicted Mother, bathed in the blood of her Son, left bereft, alone, and abandoned in this dark and sorrowful world; and as the living sparrow, seeing the blood-stains of its mate on its wings would not rest for a moment, but would fly from place to place, and at last die of terror, so Mary, beholding the marks of her dear Son's most Precious Blood on her sacred garments, pined away in most intense mortal agony. My soul, hasten and condole with thy much afflicted Mother, and in order to do so with profit to thyself, study to imitate her virtues. Among the beautiful lessons taught by Mary on this occasion, that of constancy holds a conspicuous place; yes, she was most constant. In his sufferings, Jesus was forsaken by his Apostles, and neglected by his friends. Mary alone remained with Him till death. Mothers, generally speaking, cannot see their children suffer, much less have they strength to see them die; but " Mary stood," says St. Anselm, "most constant in the faith of Jesus." "Yes," continues St. Ambrose, "the Mother stood before the cross, and stood intrepidly when the men had fled away." Oh, learn, my soul, from this noble constancy of Mary, never to let anything disturb thee in the service of God. Never suffer anything to prevent thee from performing thy duty. Love God in desolation as well as in consolation; on Calvary as well as on Tabor; crucified as well as glorified. Mary served and loved Him both in adversity and prosperity; as well when in the hands of executioners as when worshipped by the Magi. Do thou, then my soul, bear and conquer the toil of virtue; by thy constancy stand firm in spite of trouble; continue the works of piety once begun, and remain resolute in thy good purposes. Oh, Mary, most constant Virgin, and faithful Mother of God, obtain for me that with thee I may stand firmly at the foot of the cross, that nothing may cause me to desert the standard of the Holy Cross.

This I firmly resolve; yes, I sincerely purpose to be induced neither by love of life, nor fear of death, neither by threats nor promises, to be unfaithful to my God. "Who then shall separate us from the love of Christ? I am sure that neither death nor life, nor angels, nor principalities, nor powers, nor things present nor things to come, nor might, nor height, nor depth, nor any other creature, shall be able to separate us from the love of God, which is in Christ Jesus our Lord." By thy unspeakable sorrow when Jesus died, help me to keep this resolution, which through thee, most pious Lady, I have made; for thus shall I fittingly condole with thee in the death of Jesus, thy best Beloved.

PRAYER.

Behold me now, in all humility, prostrate before thy sacred feet. Melt, O Queen of Martyrs, melt, I beseech thee, my hard heart, and thaw it with those tears which I have seen thee shed beneath the cross on Calvary; so that I

Pilate the Governor, and besought him earnestly that they might do that, and take them down from the crosses on which they were suspended. "Then the Jews," says St. John, "because it was the Parasceve, that the bodies might not remain upon the crosses on the Sabbath day, besought Pilate that their legs might be broken, and that they might be taken away." Pilate consented to their request, and sent soldiers to carry it into effect.

So now I behold Mary, with fear and trembling, watch the approach of those ruffians. She knows not, indeed, what they come for, yet she is very much afraid lest their errand be to injure the corpse of her beloved Son. But soon, alas! she sees them, with iron bars in hand, go up first to one of the robbers, then to the other, and with violent strokes break to pieces their legs, already dislocated. At last they come to Jesus. . . . . They examine whether He be yet dead or not. . . . . They are ready to strike the ignominious blow. . . . . Oh,

God! Thou alone knowest what terror seizes the pure soul of thy Divine Son's Mother. Thou alone canst tell her sorrow! She fears; she trembles; her heart beats with dread lest perhaps it be the turn of Jesus to undergo that ignominy. St. Bonaventure represents her approaching to the men, and beseeching them not to injure his limbs. Hear now, my soul, this much afflicted Mother thus expostulate with them. "Cruel soldiers, why this barbarity? Why mutilate my murdered Son? Why break his limbs? He is already dead; moreover, He has never done you harm; cease, therefore, cease to maltreat Him; desist from torturing me his Mother." But whilst she thus meekly remonstrates with those men of blood, she beholds, to her unspeakable surprise and horror, one of the fierce ruffians brandishing a spear and plunging it into her Son's adorable side. She contemplates this new wound, and whilst she weeps over it, to her great amazement she perceives flowing therefrom water mingled with blood down the already crimsoned cross; and the lance by which this monstrous deed was done is deeply dyed with his Sacred Blood. "But one of the soldiers," continues the above-named Evangelist, "opened his side with a spear, and immediately there came out blood and water." Nothing can be more painful than to see the dead body of a much esteemed and guiltless relative insulted and mangled by the murderer's hand. Great, then, yea, exceedingly great must have been the affliction of Mary when she beheld this hard-hearted soldier uplift the cruel spear, take aim, and with a violent thrust pierce through the heart of her dead Jesus.

When the point of the lance transfixed the side of Jesus, He was already dead; for He had, after having commended his blessed soul to his Eternal Father, peacefully yielded up the ghost. Justly, then, may we say with St. Alphonsus and the devout Lanspergius, "that Christ divided the punishment of this wide wound with his Mother, that He might receive the injury, she the pain." And this St. Bernard confirms: "The spear," says he, "which opened Jesus' side, passed through the heart of Mary, which could not be torn from her Son." Contemplate now, my soul, this broken-hearted Mother, and condole with her as best you can. It was an excess of charity which made our Dear Lord permit his sacred side to be opened. He would spill for man's redemption the last drop of his Precious Blood, and because after his death there still remained a little blood in his heart, willingly did He suffer the lance to enter it. Oh, if I would comfort Mary now in her woe, and impart to her sad soul feelings of delight, I must imitate, as far as in me lies, the boundless charity of her dead Son. I must, like Him, after having died to myself, open wide my heart to receive all mankind, and, if God so wills, I must be ready like Jesus to shed my blood for every one. Yes, if I would soothe the pains of the Mother, my soul must possess the charity of the

Son. It behoves me, therefore, to enquire whether I have this lovely virtue, or whether I must confess that charity is dead within me. This I can easily know if I listen to St. Paul, who, in his first Epistle to the Corinthians, tells me what are the qualities which charity should have, in order to be genuine. He says, " Charity is patient, is kind : charity envieth not, dealeth not perversely, is not puffed up, is not ambitious, seeketh not her own, is not provoked to anger, thinketh no evil, rejoiceth not in iniquity, but rejoiceth with the truth, beareth all things, believeth all things, hopeth all things : charity never falleth away."

Examine thyself, my soul, by this criterion proposed by the Apostle of the Gentiles, and judge whether thou imitatest the charity of Jesus. Art thou patient with thy neighbour ? Art thou kind to him ? If not, thou dost not possess true charity. Dost thou at any time envy him or his goods? Dost thou deal perversely with him ? If so, thou hast not true charity. Art thou ever puffed up with pride, or dost thou glory or tyranically domineer over others? If so, be sure that thou dost not possess true charity. Art thou ambitious, or dost thou seek thy own interests to the prejudice of another? If so, thou hast not true charity. Art thou easily provoked to anger? If so, thy charity is not true. Art thou inclined to think evil of thy neighbour? Dost thou rejoice in his misfortunes, frailties, and sins? If so, thou hast not true charity. Dost thou rejoice with truth, and frankly acknowledge it when it is evidently brought forward? If not, thou dost not possess true charity. Dost thou take in good part the annoyances given by others? Dost thou believe in their assertions when not opposed to truth or faith? If not, thou dost not possess true charity. Dost thou hope for the best from thy neighbour, and put up with his faults and imperfections, trusting that with the aid of God's grace he will overcome them? If not, thy charity is by no means true. In fine, does it extend to all persons and to all times, both in prosperity and adversity? If not, thy charity is not pure, it is not genuine. I must, alas! confess that my love for my neighbour is very deficient in many of these qualities, and, in consequence, that I do not possess true charity. Hide thyself, therefore, my soul, in the open side of Jesus, wash thyself in that bath of water and blood which flows therefrom, and beg Him to impart that which thou canst not obtain by thy own efforts—in other words, to give thee genuine charity. And thus wilt thou wipe the tears from Mary's eyes, solace her broken heart, and heal the wounded side of Jesus.

SECOND POINT.

Whilst Mary was contemplating the wound in the side of Jesus, Joseph, a faithful and wealthy disciple of our Lord, went privately to the Roman Governor and entreated to be allowed to take the sacred Body down from the cross, in order that due respect might be paid, and that it might be buried with becoming solemnity. "After these things," says St. John, "Joseph of Arimathea besought Pilate that he might take away the Body of Jesus." Pilate having been assured, in answer to his enquiries, that Jesus was really dead, granted without further demur the desired leave, and commanded that the Body should be delivered. Wherefore Joseph hastened to Calvary, where, assisted by Nicodemus and the beloved Apostle, he took our dear Lord down from the cross.

Behold, my soul, this mournful scene! These pious men first extract the nails from the feet ; then, whilst one of them supports the hallowed Body of our Lord, the other two take out the nails which hold his sacred hands, and consign them steeped in blood to the outstretched hands of Mary, as Metaphrastes supposes them to have done. When the nails were extracted, Jesus was carefully let down from the bloodstained gibbet into the spotless lap of her who gave Him birth. Turn, therefore, thy eyes to gaze on Mary, and condole with her over the corpse of her

Beloved. In agonies of pain she contemplates his lacerated flesh and disfigured beauty. One by one, with trembling hand, she gently draws out the cruel thorns which are deeply rooted in his head. She wipes away the blood, and counts attentively his wounds; then, with indescribable tenderness and love, she fondly kisses his head, his hands, his feet; and as she does so she heaves many a sigh, and bathes and washes them with her scalding tears. Oh, well may she exclaim, in the words of the Canticles, as she fondly presses Jesus to her heart: "A bundle of myrrh is my Beloved to me; He shall abide between my breasts:" for her grief is beyond all description.

Oh! how many swords, says St. Bonaventure, wounded the soul of this Mother, when her Son taken down from the Cross was presented to her! Were a murdered and mutilated child to be presented to his mother covered with wounds and blood, she would die with grief, as indeed has often happened; so, too, Mary would have breathed her last when she held in her arms the mangled body of her dead Son, had not God preserved her life by a singular miracle. St. Bernard asks how it happened that the Blessed Virgin did not expire in the midst of such utter anguish, when we read in the 4th chapter of the 1st Book of Kings, that the wife of Phinees bowed herself down and died of sorrow, because the Ark had been taken and her husband slain. To which St. Anselm answers that "she would most certainly have died, if she had not been assisted by the Holy Ghost."

But, my soul, she speaks, and in most doleful words gives utterance to such sentiments as these: "When on earth was there anyone so cruelly treated as Thou, my innocent Son? Oh, my consolation, my only joy! Where is that happiness which I experienced at thy birth? Where the honour and dignity conferred on me by thy presence? O anguish! O bitterness! O mortal agony of heart!! But men, cruel men, you have caused it all! By your wickedness you have caused my darling Son to die. He gave Himself for your sins. 'He was wounded for your iniquities, He was bruised for your sins.' You, therefore, are his murderers." Such words of lamentation, no doubt, escaped from Mary's guileless lips, when she supported on her knees the dead Body of her beloved Son! But she speaks yet again; methinks I hear her also say to Jesus, whom she thus addresses: "Men have killed Thee, my Child! and by this act have plunged a thousand daggers in my heart; yea, in some sort, they have done me more hurt than Thee; for all thy tortures were my tortures, too; and yet, besides, I have to bear all the dread anguish that as thy Mother I alone can feel. But shall I seek revenge, or ask for mercy for thy murderers? Shall I forgive the evil done to Thee and me, or let impartial justice take its course, and let the flames of hell devour them as they deserve? Oh pardon! pardon! I ask forgiveness! Do thou forgive as I have just forgiven. When Thou wert dying, remember Thou didst pray for those who crucified Thee; with Thee, then, in behalf of wicked man, I say, 'Father, forgive them, they know not what they do;' in behalf of those who have caused my present sorrow, I crave forgiveness. Reject me not, for mercy is more thine than mine."

Consider well, my soul, this merciful conduct of Mary and learn from her forgiveness of injuries. If perchance my neighbour affronts me, or injures my reputation, I seem unable ever to forgive; even when after much demur I grant a pardon humbly asked for, I say to everyone, that I forgive but I never shall forget; and the truth of this assertion I make known by my resentment to him who gave me the offence, or by my averted looks and harsh behaviour. O Mary, how great is the distance between me and thee! I entertain animosity against my enemy; thou, merciful forgiveness. I cry out revenge; thou, pardon. And yet no one has offended me so much as I have offended thee. By my sins I have scourged thy Son at the pillar and crowned Him with thorns; by my sins I have loaded his mangled shoulders with the heavy cross, and nailed his hands and feet. Finally, by my sins I have murdered Him, pierced through his sacred side, and restored Him thus injured, bathed in blood, to thy maternal bosom. Thou didst pardon me, nevertheless, and pray for my forgiveness; and yet I will not forgive my enemies. How long shall I persist in this blind folly? How long shall I be so ungrateful to thy love? Can I expect forgiveness, if I will not forgive? Oh no, neither Jesus nor Mary will pardon me, if I do not pardon all those who have injured me. Therefore, as I desire to be forgiven, in imitation of thee, dear Mother, I do forgive all who have offended me. Pray for me, that, in this generous act, my heart may prove sincere, and that I may not only pardon but also love my enemies, in obedience to the command of thy Beloved Son. Let the wounds, the blood, and the lifeless corpse of Jesus plead in my behalf.

PRAYER.

O Queen of Martyrs, great indeed must have been thy woe, when before thy eyes the side of thy dear Son was transpierced. By the pain which thou didst then feel, by thy tears and the water and blood which flowed from this fresh wound of Jesus, I most humbly beseech thee obtain for me true charity. I pray for this, in order thereby to staunch his blood and heal thy broken heart, since I know it to be a sweet and healing balm to Jesus and to thee. But my prayer is not yet finished. When holding in thy arms the murdered body of Jesus, thou didst fervently pray for the vile and wretched men who did the bloody deed. Oh, then, I implore thee by his wounds, his pains, his blood, obtain for me the spirit of sincere forgiveness, that I may freely pardon all who have offended me. This, dear Mother, is all that I ask. Bless me, hear my prayer, and grant that one day I may come to live and

Ejaculation.

Mary, by the open side of Jesus, by his wounds, which thou didst count when thou didst hold Him dead upon thy knees, I ask the grace of charity and forgiveness; charity that I may love all for God and in God; forgiveness that I may entertain ill-will to none.

Say "three *Ave Marias* in honour of all Mary suffered on Mount Calvary, for the grace of *Perfect Contrition.*"

ON THE SEVENTH DOLOUR OF MARY.

Mary at the Burial of Jesus.

FIRST POINT.

After Jesus was taken down from the cross, his Body, as we have seen, was laid on the lap of his Mother. But, alas! Mary was not allowed this melancholy consolation long; for the dawn of the Sabbath was fast approaching, and, therefore, it became necessary to bury our Lord as soon as possible, since on the Sabbath day funerals were forbidden by the law of the ancient synagogue, which, we read in the writings of Theophylactus and St. Chrysostom, prohibited not only all ordinary manual labour on that day, but also the interment of the dead. Behold, my soul, the Blessed Virgin, on this sad and solemn occasion. She is immersed for the seventh time in an ocean of unfathomable grief. Once more does she clasp with fond embrace the body of her Son, once more does she imprint a thousand kisses on his wounds, his hands, and feet. Once more, and for the last time, she presses his transfixed side to her heart, and bathes his thorn-pierced forehead with her tears. "The most dolorous Mother," says St. Bernard, "watered the face of her Son with an abundance of tears, . . . and in the meantime she frequently kissed his cheeks, his brow, and mouth." After Mary had thus sorrowfully caressed our Lord for the last time, with wondrous fortitude, she entrusted his precious remains to the custody of Joseph of Arimathea, St. John and Nicodemus, who, as the Sacred Scriptures say, came bringing a mixture of myrrh and aloes, about a hundred pounds weight, to embalm the body. These holy disciples receive this adorable charge with all imaginable devotion and affection, embalm it with their spices, and bind it carefully in a clean linen sheet. "They, therefore, took the Body of

Jesus and bound it in linen cloths with spices, as the manner of the Jews is to bury."

Oh! methinks I see Mary, impelled by ardent love, assist in laying out her Son for the gloomy sepulchre. Yes, I behold her, her eyes streaming with tears, placing in each purple aperture of his hands and feet the bitter myrrh and aloes. Poignant, indeed, must be her grief whilst thus she is engaged—whilst thus again she numbers his sacred wounds. For, no doubt, since her pure soul was a mirror of her Son's bitter Passion, she felt in her loving heart the pain which she knew He had undergone in the several parts of his mangled Body. But if I would know better the intensity of this pain, I need but listen attentively to these words of St. Bernard, in his treatise on the lamentations of Mary: "I do not believe that the grief of the Virgin can fully be conceived, unless we believe it to be as much as such a Mother could ever possibly feel for such a Son.

Oh! indeed, it is too true, that as Mary surpassed all others in sanctity and merit, so and in the same degree did she surpass them in grief, torture, and pain." Do thou, my soul, condole with thy afflicted Mother; assist her in embalming that Body which thy sins have rendered lifeless. Kiss again and again his wounds, and anoint with penitential tears his sacred flesh. Mary, as I have seen, had the Blessed Body of Jesus embalmed with spices, and carefully wrapped in linen, clean and fine. Now, it appears to me that, even in this there is instruction for her devoted clients; for the clean linen sheet represents the virtue of holy purity; and the spices, which were myrrh and aloes, according to St. Gregory the Great, mean the assiduous practice of mortification. The clean sheet signifies purity; because, as white linen, being clean, preserves the body also clean, so does holy purity keep the soul from sinful stain. The spices represent mortification, because as myrrh and bitter aloes preserve from corruption the lifeless frame, so the practice of mortification, as the Holy Fathers explain, sustains in grace the human soul. Oh! then, Mary would have her pious children learn from the embalming of her Divine Son these two beautiful virtues, which shone forth resplendently in her own person—holy purity and mortification. My soul, what answer canst thou make for thyself? Art thou pure and chaste? Art thou truly mortified, both interiorly and exteriorly? Oh! examine thyself well, for thy salvation is in peril if thou art not; search well into thy thoughts, words, and actions; and if, perchance, thou findest that thou art not as thou shouldst be, turn to Mary, expose to her thy misfortune, and learn from her these excellent lessons of mortification and purity. She wraps up in clean white linen the Body of her lifeless Son; do thou, my soul, cover thyself with the sheet of virginal

soul, join in this melancholy procession; follow, as a mourner, the corpse of thy Redeemer, and contemplate the sorrows of his Mother.

Lo! the most loving of parents follows to the grave the most loving of sons! Mary follows Jesus! A virgin Mother! A man God! But who can tell her grief on this occasion. Parents generally feel very acute pain at the funeral of a child, particularly if that child has been marked by unusual love, beauty or intellect; they fret and weep bitterly, and, indeed, their happiness seems entirely blighted, or rather perfectly destroyed; how much, then, must not Mary have suffered, as she followed the remains of a son most affectionate—yea, than whom there was never one more loving or more dutiful. Moreover, Jesus was of all sons the most intelligent, being the Eternal Wisdom of the Father. He was also the most beautiful, his Blessed Body being formed in a most beautiful Virgin by the operation of the Holy Ghost. It was of Him the inspired David sang:

"Thou art beautiful above the sons of men; grace is poured abroad in thy lips." Certainly, therefore, the grief of Mary must have surpassed the sorrow of all other parents in a very great degree. St. Bernard says: "Man's mind cannot explain, nor can words express, how sensibly the interior of the heart of Mary was afflicted on this occasion." All that we can understand is, that when the Blessed Virgin followed Jesus to the grave, her grief must have almost reached the limits of infinitude.

When the mournful cortége reached the place appointed for the burial, the disciples of our Lord let down from their shoulders his sacred Body, and placed it in that part of the tomb prepared for its reception. At the afflicting sight, Mary's heart melted like wax before the fire. What David the prophet long before foretold in reference to the Son, may be applied to the Mother. "My heart is become like wax, melting in the midst of my bowels." We may now, therefore, say of her what Jeremias said of desolate Jerusalem : "Weeping, she hath wept in the night, and the tears are on her cheeks: there is none to comfort her among all them that were dear to her." And we may place on her most sorrowful lips these words of the Lamentations : "Behold, O Lord, for I am in distress, my bowels aré troubled : my heart is turned within me, for I am full of bitterness ; abroad the sword destroyeth, and at home there is death alike." Therefore do I weep, and my eyes run down with water : because the comforter, the relief of my soul, is far from me. "They have heard that I sigh, and there is none to comfort me." Yes, her maternal bowels are torn asunder with grief, so dire is her distress at the burial of Jesus. "Oh, how willingly would I," said she once to St. Bridget, " then have been placed with my Son, had he so willed."

It is believed by some authors that when the Body of Jesus was laid in the tomb, the Blessed Virgin accompanied into it the hallowed remains, and there deposited the nails and crown of thorns. Oh! how much more poignant must not this have made her grief, especially when the moment came that she was to separate herself from the lifeless Body of her Son. Oh! methinks I see her embrace the much loved corpse in spasms of pain. But she lingers in the cold, dark sepulchre, in an agonizing swoon—a swoon from which she recovers not until it is declared to be the will of Heaven that she should go away. Obedient to the voice, Mary tarries not a minute, but, bidding a last farewell to Jesus, she leaves at once, and then the heavy stone is dragged before the entrance, and she finds herself entirely separated from her Son. Alas! all was yet bearable while Mary had with her even the remains of her Divine Son; but when at length this sad consolation, too, was torn from her, and laid in the tomb, oh! then was the consummation of her grief; and when the sepulchre was closed by the heavy stone, and securely sealed before her eyes, oh! then, indeed, she would have died, had not God preserved her life by another miracle. "When they separated me from my buried Love, the separation wrestled with my heart like bitter death," she said herself to a faithful servant.

Oh, Mary, I do most feelingly compassionate thee in thy agonizing grief; fain would I wipe the tears away which fast fall down thy wan and wasted cheeks; fain would I console thy broken heart; but how can I do this? How relieve my Mother in her sorrow? Detachment from creatures, I think I hear her say, is the only way. It was man's vain attachment to creatures that caused all thy pain, sorrowful Mother; for had he not loved them more than he loved his God, he would not have incurred the guilt of sin, by eating the forbidden fruit of Eden, and Jesus would not have been crucified, nor wouldst thou have grieved upon his tomb; by detachment from creatures, therefore, I must repair the evil done by vile attachment to them;

for they are made not for my love, but for my use and my soul's salvation. Moreover, this is the noble example which thou, dearest Mother, didst give me at the grave of thy Beloved Son. Much, indeed, didst thou desire to watch in the sepulchre his precious remains; but when thou didst understand that Heaven wished the contrary, even from this consolation thou didst detach thy heart—yea, and without complaint; and when the great stone was rolled against the tomb, and shut thee from Jesus, thou wert resigned, and didst with the disciples of thy Son depart in peace. Oh! Mother dear, how very different is my behaviour from thine. I feel my heart attached to a thousand little trifles which I value more than God or the happiness he has promised me; and, what is most to be lamented, I know not how to detach it from them. Oh, teach me this important lesson from the emtombment of Jesus, that so this holy reflection may be to the great profit of my soul.

PRAYER.

Oh thou most afflicted yet most perfect Virgin, to thee do I confidently hasten, and in all humility cast myself at thy sacred feet. Behold me, dearest Mother, with tears of condolence compassionating thee and begging a share in thy seventh sorrow, the interment of thy Son. Oh! would that I could conceive how dire was its poignancy, would that I could fathom that sea of woe in which this Dolour plunged thy maternal heart! But, if this is not given me to know, it follows not that I cannot understand the lesson which thou didst teach me at the tomb. Thou there wert detached even from thy Son, thy best Beloved. Oh, then! obtain for me the grace to detach my heart from creatures, especially from all carnal pleasures. I am grieved indeed exceedingly for my too great love for them; now I resolve to attach my soul to God alone. This is my determined resolution; render it efficacious by thy prayers and blessing. O most clement! O most pious! O most sweet Virgin Mary! Amen.

Ejaculation.

Mary, mirror of thy dear Son's Passion, by his embalmed remains and the grave in which they were deposited, obtain for me these three virtues—Purity, Mortification, and Detachment from creatures.

Say "three *Ave Marias* in honour of all the Blessed Virgin suffered at the sepulchre of Jesus, for the grace of a *Happy Death.*"

THE END OF THE FIRST PART.

PART THE SECOND.

DEVOUT PRAYERS IN HONOUR OF THE SEVEN DOLOURS.

V. O God, stretch forth to aid me.
R. O Lord, make haste to help me.
Glory be to the Father, etc.

I. O most sorrowful Mary, I compassionate the grief of thy tender heart at the prophecy of Simeon. O beloved Mother, through that afflicted heart obtain for me the virtue of humility and the gift of the fear of God. Hail Mary.

II. O most sorrowful Mary, I compassionate those afflictions which thy most sensitive heart endured during the flight into Egypt and thy dwelling there. O beloved Mother, by that afflicted heart obtain for me the virtue of liberality, specially towards the poor, and the gift of pity. Hail Mary.

III. O most sorrowful Mary, I

compassionate that intense distress which thine anxious heart experienced in the loss of thy dearest Jesus. O beloved Mother, by that deeply-troubled heart obtain for me the virtue of chastity and the gift of knowledge. Hail Mary.

IV. O most sorrowful Mary, I compassionate the consternation which thy maternal heart experienced when thou didst see Jesus bearing the cross. O beloved Mother, of thy tender heart obtain for me the virtue of patience and the gift of fortitude. Hail Mary.

V. O most sorrowful Mary, I compassionate that martyrdom which thy generous heart endured in witnessing the last agony of Jesus. O beloved Mother, by that martyred heart obtain for me the virtue of temperance and the gift of counsel. Hail Mary.

VI. O most sorrowful Mary, I compassionate that wound which thy mournful heart endured from the lance which tore the side of Jesus and wounded his heart. O beloved

Mother, by thy pierced heart obtain for me the virtue of fraternal charity and the gift of understanding. Hail Mary.

VII. O most sorrowful Mary, I compassionate the convulsions which thy most loving heart experienced at the burial of Jesus. O beloved Mother, by this extreme grief of thy sacred heart obtain for me the virtue of diligence and the gift of wisdom. Hail Mary.

V. Pray for us, O Dolorous Virgin Mother of God.

R. That we may be made worthy of the promises of Christ.

Let us Pray.

Grant we beseech thee, O Lord Jesus Christ, that the Blessed Virgin Mary, thy Mother, may intercede for us with thy clemency, now and at the hour of our death; who, at the time of thy Passion, was transfixed in her most holy soul by seven swords of sorrow; grant us this great blessing, O Jesus Christ, Saviour of the world, who with the Father and the Holy Ghost livest and reignest ever, world without end. Amen.

NOTE.—A perpetual indulgence of 300 days applicable to the dead, to all Christians every time they recite the above exercise in honour of *Mary's Woes.*

ROSARY OF THE SEVEN DOLOURS OF THE BLESSED VIRGIN MARY.

I. The heartrending anguish which Mary felt in her pure soul when she heard from the prophetic lips of Holy Simeon the future sufferings of her Son.

One Our Father and seven Hail Marys.

II. The sword of grief which transfixed Mary's heart during the flight into Egypt.

One Our Father and seven Hail Marys.

III. Mary's misery and woe when Jesus was lost for three days.

One Our Father and seven Hail Marys.

IV. Mary meets Jesus carrying his cross, and she faints at his feet.

One Our Father and seven Hail Marys.

V. Mary stands beneath the cross, beholds Him die, and falls into the arms of St. John, with a broken heart.

One Our Father and seven Hail Marys.

VI. Mary recovers from her swoon, and receives on her lap the corpse of her Son.

One Our Father and seven Hail Marys.

VII. Mary with tears in her eyes follows her Son to the tomb and sees Him buried.

One Our Father and seven Hail Marys.

In honour of the tears Mary shed during her Dolours.

Three Hail Marys.

V. Pray for us, O sorrowful Mother of Jesus.

R. That we may be made worthy of the promises of Christ.

PRAYER.

Grant, we beseech Thee, O Lord Jesus Christ, that the Blessed Virgin thy Mother may intercede for us with thy clemency, now and at the hour of our death; who, in the hour of thy Passion, was pierced in her most holy soul by a sword of sorrow; grant this, O Jesus Christ, Saviour of the world, who livest and reignest with the Father and the Holy Ghost, world without end. Amen.

INDULGENCES FOR THE ABOVE ROSARY.

I. 200 days for each Our Father and Hail Mary, when recited in the churches of the Order of the Servants of Mary.

II. 200 days for each Our Father and Hail Mary, when recited on Friday, on all the days of Lent, and on the Feast and Octave of the Seven Dolours, in any place whatever.

III. 100 days for each recital, in any place or at any time, together with seven years and seven quarantines.

IV. Plenary, with confession and communion, for those who have said it daily for a month.

V. 100 years for each recital.

VI. 150 years for Mondays, Wednesdays, and Fridays.

VII. Plenary once a year for those who recite it at least four times a week.

VIII. 200 years for those who recite it after confession.

IX. For those who frequently recite this Rosary, and have one about their persons, an indulgence of ten years each time they assist at Mass, hear sermons, accompany the Blessed Sacrament to the sick, bring sinners to repentance, &c., &c.; and the same indulgence for those who perform some spiritual or corporal work in honour of our Blessed Lord, the Blessed Virgin, or their patron Saints, reciting at the same time seven Our Fathers and seven Hail Marys.

All these indulgences are applicable to the dead.

LITANY OF THE SEVEN DOLOURS OF THE BLESSED VIRGIN.

Lord have mercy on us. *Lord have mercy on us.*
Christ have mercy on us. *Christ have mercy on us.*
Lord have mercy on us. *Lord have mercy on us.*
Christ hear us. *Christ graciously hear us.*
God the Father of Heaven,
God the Son, Redeemer of the World,
God the Holy Ghost,
Holy Trinity, one God, *Have mercy on us.*
Mother of Dolours, *Pray for us.*
Thou who didst find no room in the inn,
Who wast forced to take refuge in a stable,
Who didst lay thy first-born in a manger,
Who didst witness the circumcision of thy Son,
Who didst hear that thy Son was set as a sign that should be contradicted, *Pray for us.*

Who didst hear that thy own soul should be pierced with a sword,
Who didst fly into Egypt with thy Son,
Who didst grieve for the murder of the Innocents,
Who for three days didst seek sorrowing thy Son, lost in the Temple when He was twelve years old,
Who didst note the constant hatred of the Jews against Him,
Who on the day of the last Supper didst bid farewell to thy Son going to Jerusalem to die.
Who didst learn that He was betrayed by Judas, and led away captive,
Who didst see Him delivered up as a malefactor by the chief priests,
Who didst hear that He was falsely accused,
Who didst learn that his blessed face was struck,
Who didst learn that He was most cruelly treated by the Jews and the soldiers,

Pray for us.

Who didst hear thy Son rejected for Barabbas,
Who didst behold Him beaten with scourges and crowned with thorns,
Who didst hear sentence pronounced against Him,
Who didst go to meet thy Son loaded with the Cross,
Who didst see his blessed hands and feet pierced with nails,
Who didst receive the last words of Jesus upon the Cross,
Who didst stand by Him in his agony,
Who didst receive into thy bosom the lifeless Body of thy Son taken down from the Cross,
Who after the Body of Jesus was buried didst return home all sad and desolate.
O Queen of Martyrs,
O Mirror of the afflicted,
O Comfort of the weak,
O Strength of the fearful,
O Refuge of Sinners.
Through the most bitter Passion and Death of thy Son,

Pray for us.

Deliver us from sin and evil, O Queen of Martyrs.
Through the most poignant sorrow of thy heart,
Through thy exceeding sadness and desolation,
Through thy extreme anguish,
Through thy groans and tears,
Through thy maternal compassion,
Through thy most powerful patronage,
From immoderate sadness,
From a pusillanimous spirit,
From every occasion and danger of sin,
From the snares of the devil,
From hardness of heart,
From impenitence,
From sudden and unprovided death,
From eternal damnation,
We sinners,
Beseech thee hear us.
That thou wouldst vouchsafe to preserve us by thy patronage in true faith, hope, and charity,
We beseech thee hear us.
That thou wouldst vouchsafe to ob-

tain for us perfect sorrow and
repentance for our sins,
That thou wouldst vouchsafe to
bring consolation and assistance
to those who call upon thee,
That thou wouldst vouchsafe to
succour us in the agony of death,
That thou wouldst vouchsafe to
obtain for us a happy death,
Mother of God,
We beseech thee hear us.
Lamb of God, who takest away the
sins of the world,
Spare us, O Lord.
Lamb of God, who takest away the
sins of the world,
Graciously hear us, O Lord.
Lamb of God, who takest away the
sins of the world,
Have mercy on us, O Lord.
Christ hear us,
Christ graciously hear us.
Lord have mercy on us,
Christ have mercy on us.
Lord have mercy on us.
V. In all our tribulations and afflictions,
R. Succour us, O Virgin Mary,

PRAYER.

Write, O afflicted Mother, on my repentant heart thy Seven Dolours and the five bleeding Wounds which thy dear Son bore, that I may read therein sorrow and true love; sorrow, to endure for Jesus and for thee every sorrow; love, to despise every love for Him and for thee. Live, crucified Jesus and heartbroken Mary, for ever and ever! Through the same Jesus Christ our Lord. Amen.

Memorare Triste.

Remember, O Virgin Mary, most sorrowful of the afflicted daughters of suffering Eve, that from all ages it has never been known that anyone imploring thy assistance failed to gain thy compassion and protection. Animated with the confidence which this inspires, to thee, O Queen of Martyrs and Virgin Mother, I come, as a contrite sinner, weeping and kneeling. Do not, O Mother of Jesus crucified, despise my suppliant voice, but hear and grant my prayer. Amen.

THE WAY OF THE MOTHER;
OR,
THE SEVEN DOLOURS OF MARY.
IN THE SAME FORM AS
THE WAY OF THE CROSS.
From the Italian.

Invitation to the Faithful.

Whatever act of homage is practised by the faithful in honour of the Blessed Virgin is welcomed by her with singular love, but above all she is pleased at seeing us occupied in compassionating her Dolours. Such a devotion is so gratifying to Mary, that when she found it in the time of St. Bridget very much neglected, she complained to her in these words:— "Pauci sunt qui recogitent dolorem meum." "There are few who remember my sorrows."

Wherefore, in order to assist you

in meditating upon the Dolours of Mary, we propose to you this devout exercise of the Stations of her Seven Dolours, which can be practised in public or private, in the same manner as the Way of the Cross.

This holy exercise has been instituted for some time, and is every day spreading. It was publicly practised in Rome A.D. 1836, in the Church of St. Marcellus, and has been enriched by copious Indulgences of the holy memory of Gregory XVI. A Plenary Indulgence was granted, on July 31st, 1837, to those who on any day shall visit seven times the Stations of the Dolours, and for each time seven years' Indulgence.

THE WAY OF THE MOTHER;

OR,

THE SEVEN DOLOURS OF THE VIRGIN MARY.

IN THE SAME FORM AS

THE WAY OF THE CROSS.

V. Come Holy Ghost, replenish the hearts of the faithful.

R. And enkindle in them the fire of thy love.

V. Send forth thy spirit, O Lord, and they shall be regenerated.

R. And Thou shalt renew the face of the earth.

V. Remember thy congregation.

R. Which Thou hast possessed from the beginning.

V. Lord, hear my prayer.

R. And let my cry come unto Thee.

V. The Lord be with thee.

R. And with thy spirit.

Act of Contrition.

Oh most afflicted Virgin! Alas, with what unthankfulness in my past life have I acted towards God! with what ingratitude have I corresponded to his innumerable benefits! Now, however, I am truly penitent, and in the bitterness of my heart and the sorrow of my soul, I humbly beg pardon for having outraged his infinite bounty, resolving for the future, by his grace, never more to offend Him. Oh! by all the Dolours which thou hast borne in the Passion of Jesus, I pray thee with tears to implore from Him pity and mercy for my many grievous sins. Receive this holy devotion, which I am about to perform, in memory of those pains and Dolours. Grant! oh grant that those seven daggers which pierced through thy soul may likewise pierce through mine, and that I may live and die in the friendship of the Lord, and enjoy eternally the glory which He has acquired for me by his most precious Blood. Amen.

among the ungrateful. Throw thyself at the feet of thy sorrowful Mother, and weeping pray to her thus: Oh most dear Virgin Mary, thou who didst experience spasms of pain in thy soul at seeing the abuse that I, an unworthy creature, have made of the precious fountains of thy Blessed Son's Blood; grant! oh grant, by the sorrows of thy afflicted heart, that for the future I may correspond to divine mercy, may not abuse grace, nor receive so many lights in vain, but may, by the assistance of Divine grace, have the happy lot to be ranked among the number of the elect, for whom the Passion of Jesus will obtain eternal happiness. Amen. *Ave Maria.*

Most sorrowful Virgin, pray for us.

O Mary, sweetness of my life,
Stamp on my soul thy bitter strife,
And pray for me, that I may see
Thy joys for all eternity.

STATION I.

FIRST DOLOUR.

In this first Dolour imagine thyself, oh my soul, standing in the Temple of Jerusalem, when the Blessed Virgin heard the prophecy of Holy Simeon.

Meditation.

Ah! how broken must have been the heart of Mary when she listened to the words by which Holy Simeon predicted the bitter Passion and death of Jesus; for at that moment she beheld in her mind all those affronts, blows, and lacerations that the Redeemer of the world would have to bear from the impious Jews. But which of those was the most afflicting on this sad occasion? It was the consideration of the ingratitude with which her Son would be requited by men. Oh! reflect, my soul, that by reason of thy sins thou also wert

felt at the first gaze which she fixed on her suffering Child. She wished to give Him the last farewell, but the sorrow which oppressed her prevented her from uttering a word; she tried to throw herself upon his neck, but could not move, and, petrified with grief, she tried to cry, but could not shed a tear. Oh! who can refrain from weeping at seeing a poor mother so overwhelmed with sorrow? But who has been the cause of such sharp pain? Ah! it is I who by my grievous sins have cruelly wounded the tender heart of Mary. Can I, then, remain insensible and not repent of my inhuman cruelty?

Oh! holy Virgin, I beg thee to pardon me the grievous pains which I have caused to thee. I know and I confess that I merit no pity, because I was the true cause of thy affliction in this sorrowful meeting with thy Son; but remember that thou art the Mother of Mercy. Ah! shew, then, some mercy towards me, and I promise for the future to be more faithful to my Redeemer, and thus to compensate the many pangs and sufferings which I have caused thee. Amen. *Ave Maria.*

Virgin most sorrowful, pray for us.

O Mary, sweetness of my life,
Stamp on my soul thy bitter strife,
And pray for me, that I may see
Thy joys for all eternity.

STATION V.

FIFTH DOLOUR.

In this fifth Dolour, imagine thyself, oh my soul, on the heights of Calvary when the most afflicted Virgin saw her beloved Son die.

Meditation.

Come, oh devout soul! come to Calvary, where are being offered to God two sacrifices; one is the Body of Jesus, the other is the heart of Mary. Oh! sorrowful spectacle, to look upon this good Mother in such a sea of woe—beholding Him, who is more dear to her than life itself, martyred by the most cruel death. Alas! every blow of the hammer, every wound, every laceration which the Saviour of the world received on his sacred Body, Mary received upon her heart. She stood there at the foot of the cross, so penetrated with pain and transfixed with such agony that it could not be decided which should be the first to expire—

Jesus or Mary. Fixing her eyes on her Blessed Son she sees that He is already breathing forth his last breath; she gazes upon his sunken eyes, his ghastly looks, his livid lips, and listens to his difficult breathing, and at last she knows that He no longer lives, and that He has already yielded his blessed spirit to his Eternal Father. Ah! surely she wished that at that moment her soul could be separated from her body and united to the soul of Jesus. And who could bear such a sight as this? Oh, most afflicted of all mothers! instead of returning from Calvary to be free from such bitter suffering, thou didst remain there immovable as a rock in order to drink to the last drop the chalice of thy affliction. What confusion must this be for me, my soul, who strive in every way to remove those little crosses and light sufferings which God thinks fit to send me for my greater good. Grant! oh grant that I may know the value of sufferings and that I may become so attached to them, that not being satisfied with those thou sendest to me, I may cry out with St. Francis Xavier, "Plura, Domine, plura:" "More sufferings, oh my God—oh yes, more sufferings." Amen. *Ave Maria.*

Virgin most sorrowful, pray for us.

O Mary, sweetness of my life,
Stamp on my soul thy bitter strife,
And pray for me, that I may see
Thy joys for all eternity.

STATION VI.

SIXTH DOLOUR.

In this sixth Dolour contemplate, oh my soul, the Blessed Virgin when she received into her arms her dead Son after He was taken down from the cross.

Meditation.

Consider the pang which penetrated the heart of Mary when she held in her arms the dead Body of her Son. Ah! when she fixed her weeping eyes upon his gaping wounds, when she counted his sorrows and saw Him shedding so much blood, how terrific must have been the shock to her mind, and how deadly the blow which broke her sacred heart; and, indeed, she would have fallen down dead, through agony, but for the assistance of Divine power. Oh poor Mother! yes, Mother of Martyrs, thou didst bear to the tomb the dear object of thy most tender care, who, from being fair as the rose, became like to a bed of thorns by the ill-treatment and lacerations given by the executioners. And who would not pity thee, who would not feel themselves struck by sorrow at seeing thee in sorrow, such as would move to pity the most stony heart? I behold St. John inconsolable, Mary Magdalen with the other Marys in bitterest grief, Nicodemus not able to stand under his afflictions. And I, alas! I alone cannot shed a tear in the midst of such sorrow, ungrateful and unthankful creature that I am. Oh, my dear Mother Mary, grant that my heart may be transfixed by those same daggers which passed through thy most afflicted heart, and that I may now become truly penitent for those sins which caused thee such a cruel martyrdom. Amen. *Ave Maria.*

Virgin most sorrowful, pray for us.

O Mary, sweetness of my life,
Stamp on my soul thy bitter strife,
And pray for me, that I may see
Thy joys for all eternity.

STATION VII.

SEVENTH DOLOUR.

In this seventh Dolour, contemplate, oh my soul, the most sorrowful Virgin at the Sepulchre of her dead Son.

Meditation.

Consider how full of woe must have been the sigh which the most afflicted heart of Mary sent forth when she placed in the tomb her amiable Jesus. Oh! what pain, what great woe, must she have felt in her soul, when she beheld the rock lifted with which that sacred monument was to be closed; she could not be separated from the side of the sepulchre, and her sorrow was such that it rendered her immovable, nor was she ever satisfied with looking at those cruel wounds. And when the tomb was closed, so great was her grief that she could hardly live.

Oh! most cruelly-tortured Mother,

thou wilt depart presently in body from this place, but here will thy heart remain with thy true treasure. Oh grant that here too all my affections and my love may rest. How is it possible not to be struck with love for the Saviour who has given his Precious Blood for our salvation? And how is it possible not to love thee, who hast suffered so much for love of us? Oh! by all thy Dolours upon which we have meditated, grant this favour, that the memory of those pains may always remain impressed upon our minds, that our poor hearts may be inflamed with love of God and thee, most sweet Mother, and that the last sighs of our lives may be united to those which thou didst send forth from the depth of thy heart at the Passion of Jesus; to whom be honour, glory, and thanks for ever and ever. Amen. *Ave Maria.*

Virgin most sorrowful, pray for us.

O Mary, sweetness of my life,
Stamp on my soul thy bitter strife,

And pray for me, that I may see
Thy joys for all eternity.

At the end, returning to the altar, say one part of the Stabat Mater.

V. Pray for us, O Virgin most sorrowful.

R. That we may be made worthy of the promises of Christ.

Prayer.

O God, in whose Passion, according to the prophecy of Simeon, the sword of sorrow pierced the soul of thy most glorious Mother, the Virgin Mary, mercifully grant that we who meditate upon her Dolours may obtain happiness by the effects of thy Passion. Amen.

A SHORT METHOD OF MEDITATING ON THE SEVEN DOLOURS.

I. Place yourself in spirit at the feet of the Queen of Martyrs, and offer her your meditation.

II. Ask her blessing and assistance.

III. Think what Mary suffers in the Dolour on which you wish to meditate.

IV. Think who Mary is that suffers.

V. Think why Mary suffers.

VI. Think how Mary suffers.

VII. Think how you suffer.

VIII. Think which is the principal virtue taught by Mary in that Dolour upon which you are meditating.

IX. Think whether you practice that virtue or not; if not, beg pardon of God, and promise amendment.

X. Finish by making some very practical resolutions, and by praying to Mary for relief in all your wants, both spiritual and temporal.

Prayer to the Most Desolate Virgin.

Hail Mary, full of sorrows, the Crucified is with thee ; most sorrowful art thou amongst women, and most sorrowful is the fruit of thy womb, Jesus. Holy Mary, Mother of the Crucified, beg tears for us, the crucifiers of thy Son, now and in the hour of our death. Amen.

An Indulgence of 100 days was granted by his Holiness Pius IX., on December 23rd, 1847, for each recital of this prayer.

OF THE SCAPULAR,

AND OF

THE ROSARY OF OUR LADY OF SEVEN DOLOURS.

HISTORICAL SKETCH.[*]

Devotion to our Blessed Lady is as ancient as the Church herself. But the long wars and dissensions which had desolated Europe, the ignorance, neglect of duties, and the consequent brutality of manners which ensued from this state of things, had greatly diminished it. However, an immense number of miracles which took place in the early part of the thirteenth century, communicated to it a new vigour and a wider extension. The instruments of mercy which the Blessed Virgin made use of to produce this effect were

---

[*] See Manual on Scapulars, translated by F. Raphael, Passionist.

the Rosary, which was revealed to St. Dominick, in the year 1206, and the Scapulars of the Seven Dolours and of Mount Carmel, the first of which she herself gave to the seven Founders of the Order of Servites, and the second to St. Simon Stock. In the year 1233 seven noblemen of the city of Florence, whose names were Buonfiglio Monaldi, Buonagiunta Manetti, Manetto dell' Antella, Amedeo degli Amidei, Ugiccione Uguccioni, Tostegno de' Tostegni, and Alexis Falconieri, members of a pious Confraternity for honouring the Blessed Virgin, had assembled on the festival of the Assumption, to pay their homage and celebrate her triumph. At one and the same time the Mother of God appeared to each, and told them that they were to quit the world, and embrace a more perfect state of life. They did not hesitate to obey this heavenly voice, and having consulted with the blessed Ardingo, Bishop of Florence, as to the mode of life which they should adopt, they renounced their dignities, distributed their goods to the poor, and clothed themselves in grey habits, and retired to a small house outside the town, on the feast of the Nativity of their holy Patroness (8th September, 1233).

If, at any time, they were obliged to enter the city of Florence, in order to consult the Bishop, the people assembled about them in crowds, and the little children used to exclaim, "Here are the servants of Mary! Here are the servants of Mary!" Amongst these children was St. Philip Benizzi, who was then hardly five months old, and who, in after years, was called by our Blessed Lady to assume the habit of her servants.

This humble retreat of the seven Solitaries soon became so besieged by visitors, that they were obliged to look out for a more retired place.

Their good Mother indicated to them the summit of Mount Jenario, where they removed and passed six years, principally occupied about their own sanctification, in the practice of the most austere penance, and assiduous meditation on the Passion of our Lord, and on the Dolours of his Blessed Mother. The venerable Bishop Ardingo had more than once exhorted them to establish an Order devoted to the Blessed Virgin, but in vain. The co-operation of heaven became necessary to overcome the diffidence of these holy men, and triumph over their humility.

On the evening of one Good Friday, whilst they were absorbed in profound meditation, they saw their august patroness descending from heaven, surrounded by a number of heavenly spirits, some of whom carried the instruments of the Passion; another, the rules of St. Augustine; one amongst them had in his hand a palm; another a scroll, on which the following words were engraven in golden letters, "Servants of Mary." Finally there was one who carried in his hands a black habit of a new form.

The seven anchorites, filled with astonishment at this glorious apparition, waited respectfully for the Blessed Virgin to make known her will. Mary, in the attitude of a Mother overwhelmed with affliction, and, at the same time, full of maternal tenderness, approached them, and, pointing to the objects placed before their eyes, said : " Receive this habit which I present to you, and receive also the rule of St. Augustine, which you are to follow, so that, being designated by the name of my servants, you may one day obtain the palm of eternal life offered to you."

The holy Solitaries immediately adopted the habit of their new Institute, by the spirit of which they, and so many of the faithful, were to be sanctified, through the continual meditation on the Passion of Jesus Christ, and on the bitter sorrows of his Holy Mother.

In order that all the world might be able to clothe themselves in the livery of the Servants of Mary, they instituted a smaller habit of the same form, material, and colour, with that of the religious of the Order, and desiring also to give to the faithful an easy method of honouring the principal Dolours of

Mary, they instituted a Rosary divided into seven parts, each of which is composed of one Pater and seven Aves.

Mary promised to the seven holy founders, and more particularly to the Blessed Alexis, to protect in a special manner, on all occasions, but particularly at the hour of death, those who honour her Dolours.

But if we desire to secure this precious protection of the Blessed Virgin Mary, we must not be satisfied with meditating at long intervals on her Dolours, and with wearing the habit of mourning which reminds us of them. Our compassion, if it be a true one, ought to cause us to avoid that which is the true cause of her sorrow—that is to say, everything that offends God.

OBLIGATIONS AND PRACTICES OF PIETY.

The faithful who wear the Scapular of our Blessed Lady, are not bound by any particular obligation in order to gain the Indulgences attached.

The visit to some Church of the Order, one of the conditions requisite for certain Indulgences, may be commuted by a confessor for any other pious work, when there is any infirmity or hindrance of a grave nature, which prevents such a visit being made; such for instance would be the too great distance from the church, and in such a case it would be well to ask the confessor to appoint in its place some other sanctuary, as for instance a parish church.

This faculty of commutation was granted by a brief of Clement XIII., on the 17th August, 1762. If there be any Confraternity of the Seven Dolours established in the place, they ought to endeavour to fulfil their obligations, the principal of which are to assist at the public exercises of the Confraternity ; to say daily seven Paters and Aves in memory of the Dolours of the Mother of God, and to repeat the same prayers at the death of any member of the association, for the repose of his soul. Lastly, the frequent recital of the Rosary is recommended.

INDULGENCES

ATTACHED TO THE

SCAPULAR OF THE DOLOURS.

Plenary Indulgences.

I. On the day on which the Scapular is received.

II. At the hour of death, by invoking by tongue or in heart the Holy Name of Jesus.

III. The day on which a member makes an hour's spiritual exercise in honour of the Dolours.

IV. By assisting at the monthly procession, or by fulfilling what is appointed by the confessor in place of said procession.

V. Once in the month for those who repeat daily three Paters in memory of our Saviour's Passion, and three Aves in commemoration of the Dolours, for those that are in their last agony.

VI. Once in the month also for those who say every day seven Hail Marys and the verse :—

"Holy Mary, pierce me through,
In my heart each wound renew,
Of my Saviour crucified."

VII. During the Forty Hours Devotion.
VIII. Passion Sunday.
IX. Feast of the Seven Dolours.
X. The Saturday following the Commemoration of the Seven Dolours.
XI. The Annunciation of the Blessed Virgin Mary.
XII. The Assumption of our Blessed Lady.

PARTIAL INDULGENCES.

I. Seven years and seven quarantines on the Feast of Christmas, the Annunciation, the Purification, the Assumption, and all Fridays throughout the year, by reciting five Our

Fathers and five Hail Marys in memory of the Passion.

II. Five years and as many quarantines, when members accompany the Blessed Sacrament to the sick.

III. Three hundred days once a day for those who say seven Hail Marys, followed by the verse Holy Mother, &c.

IV. One hundred and fifty days every time they meditate on the Passion or on the Dolours, and say seven Our Fathers and seven Hail Marys with the "Stabat Mater," or perform the spiritual exercises practised in the Churches of the Servites.

V. One hundred days for those who recite the "Stabat Mater."

VI. Sixty days for each work of Charity.

THE FORMULA FOR BLESSING

THE

BLACK SCAPULAR AND ROSARY

OF

OUR LADY OF THE SEVEN DOLOURS.

The priest, with the stole on, turning to the person, says :—

V. Adjutorium nostrum in nomine Domini.
R. Qui fecit cœlum et terram.
V. Dominus vobiscum.
R. Et cum spiritu tuo.

Oremus.

Omnipotens sempiterne Deus, qui morte Unigeniti tui mundum collapsum restaurare dignatus es, ut nos a morte æterna liberares, et ad gaudia regni cœlestis perduceres; respice, quæsumus, super hanc familiam servorum tuorum in nomine Beatissimæ Virginis Septem Doloribus sauciæ congregatam, de cujus gremio hic famulus tuus (vel hæc famula tua) esse cupit (vel hi famuli tui esse cupiunt), ut augeatur numerus tibi fideliter servientium et omnibus sæculi et carnis perturbationibus liberatus (vel liberata seu liberati) et a laqueis diaboli securus (vel secura seu securi), intercessione ejusdem Beatæ Mariæ Virginis, Beatorum Patrum Ordinis Fundatorum vera gaudia possideat. Per Christum Dominum nostrum. R. Amen.

Conversus ad habitum super Altare positum, Sacerdos dicit :—

Oremus.

Domine Jesu Christe, qui tegmen nostræ mortalitatis induere dignatus es; obsecramus immensam largitatis tuæ abundantiam, ut hoc genus vestimentorum quod Sancti Patres nostri ad innocentiæ humilitatisque indicium in memoriam Septem Dolorum Beatæ

Virginis Mariæ nos ferre sanxerunt, ita bene ✠ dicere digneris ut qui illis fuerit indutus (vel induta seu fuerint induti) corpore pariter et animo induat (seu induant) te Salvatorem nostrum. Qui vivis et regnas in sæcula sæculorum. R. Amen.

He then sprinkles the Scapular with holy water, saying :—Asperges me, Domine, hyssopo et mundabor : lavabis me et super nivem dealbabor.

He then blesses the Rosary of the Seven Dolours, saying :—

Oremus.

Omnipotens et misericors Deus, qui propter nimiam charitatem qua dilexisti nos, Filium tuum Unigenitum Dominum nostrum Jesum Christum pro redemptione nostra de cœlis ad terram descendere, carnem suscipere et Crucis tormentum subire voluisti ; obsecramus immensam clementiam tuam, ut hanc coronam (vel has coronas) in memoriam Septem Dolorum Genitricis ejusdem Filii tui ab Ecclesia tua fideli dicatam (vel dicatas) bene ✠ dicas, sancti ✠ fices et ei (vel eis) tantam Spiritus Sancti virtutem infundas, ut quicunque eam recitaverit (vel recitaverint) atque in domo sua reverenter tenuerit (vel tenuerint) ab omni hoste visibili et invisibili semper et ubique in hoc sæculo liberetur (vel liberentur) et in exitu suo a Beatissima Virgine Maria tibi bonis operibus coronatus (vel coronata seu coronati) præsentari mereatur (vel mereantur). Per eumdem Christum Dominum nostrum. R. Amen.

He then sprinkles the Rosary with holy water, saying :—Asperges me, etc.

Then the priest places the Habit on each whilst on their knees, saying :—
Accipe, carissime Frater (vel carissima Soror) habitum Beatæ Mariæ Virginis, singulare signum servorum suorum, in memoriam Septem Dolorum, quos in vita et morte Unigeniti Filii sui sustinuit; ut ita indutus (vel induta) sub ejus patrocinio perpetuo vivas. R. Amen.

In giving the Rosary, he says :—

Accipe Coronam Beatæ Mariæ Virginis, in memoriam Septem Dolorum suorum contextam; ut dum eam ore laudaveris, ejus pœnas toto corde compatiaris.

He then blesses the person, saying:—

Benedictio Dei Omnipotentis, Patris et Fi ✠ lii et Spiritus Sancti descendat super te (vel vos) et maneat semper. Passio Domini nostri Jesu Christi et compassio Beatæ Mariæ Virginis sit in corde et corpore nostro. R. Amen.

The manner of granting the Plenary Indulgence and the Papal Blessing to the Members of the Confraternity of the Seven Dolours in their last agony.

Dicto Confiteor, &c.

Dominus noster Jesus Christus, Filius Dei vivi, qui beato Petro Apostolo suo dedit potestatem ligandi atque absolvendi, per suam piissimam miseri-

fessionem tuam, et remittat tibi omnia peccata quæ quomodocumque in toto vitæ decursu commisisti, de quibus contritus et ore confessus es, restituens tibi stolam primam, quam in baptismate recipisti; et per indulgentiam plenariam a Summo Pontifice Paulo V. confratribus Societatis dolorum Beatæ Mariæ Virginis in articulo mortis constitutis concessam, liberet te a præsentis et futuræ vitæ pœnis, dignetur purgatorii cruciatus remittere, portas inferni claudere, Paradisi januas aperire, teque ad gaudia sempiterna perducere. Qui cum Patre et Spiritu Sancto Deus unus vivit, et regnat in sæcula sæculorum. Amen.

Oremus.

Interveniat pro hoc famulo tuo infirmo, quæsumus, Domine Jesu Christe, nunc et in hora mortis suæ apud tuam clementiam Beata Virgo Maria Mater tua, cujus sacratissimam animam in hora tuæ passionis doloris gladius pertransivit. Qui cum Patre et Spiritu Sancto vivis et regnas in sæcula sæculorum. Amen.

DEVOTION OF ST. PAUL OF THE CROSS

TOWARDS

THE DOLOURS OF THE BLESSED VIRGIN MARY.

Extract from the Life of Saint Paul of the Cross, Founder of the Congregation of the Most Holy Cross and Passion of our Lord Jesus Christ.

The Dolours of Mary, in particular, were most vividly and profoundly imprinted in his heart. He always wore round his neck the devout little habit of our Lady of Sorrows, and in Missions fervently promoted the devotion to her Dolours. Though he was not in the habit of making processions, he sometimes, to increase devotion in the people towards the sorrows of our dear Lady, took them in procession to some church where our Lady of Sorrows is venerated.

This he did at Ischia, the first time he gave a Mission there.

With all the people, he went to visit the Church of the Servants of Mary, and, on arriving at the church door, made a very fervent discourse, wept bitterly, and severely disciplined himself. Compunction and tears were general amongst the people, and from that time sprang up a new fervour of filial devotion, and of tender loving compassion for our Lady of Sorrows, which remains even to this day.

To all, generally, he recommended meditation on the Dolours with great fervour. With the same zeal with which he promoted the remembrance of our Lord's Passion, he promoted the devotion to the Dolours; for, as he said himself, if we go to the Cross, there is the Mamma; where the Mamma is, there is the Son. It was certainly enough to soften the hardest hearts to hear him speak of the bitter Dolours of Mary. He meditated and considered them with filial piety, great compassion and devotion. He sometimes imagined tender dialogues between the loving Mother and the suffering Son; but with such deep feeling that the hearers were dissolved in tears of compassion and grief. He compared the sufferings of the Son and the griefs of the Mother, to two seas, and said that we pass from the first to the second. "The grief of Mary (these are his words) is like the Mediterranean Sea; for it is written: 'Magna est velut mare contritio tua:' from this sea we pass to the other boundless sea of the Passion of Jesus, in whose person David says, 'Veni in altitudinem maris;' and here the soul enriches herself, and fishes up most precious pearls of the virtues of Jesus and Mary.' With the passion of Jesus he had always in his mouth the Dolours of Mary, and said, that his hopes lay in the Passion of the Son, and in the sorrows of the Mother. Though he spoke of them constantly, he always seemed to say something new, because he always spoke of them with new affection, so deeply was he penetrated with them in his heart. Most frequently when he spoke thus, he wept bitterly, and changed colour, becoming first red, then pale; he then burst forth into these words, which came from the profoundest depths of his heart: "Ah, poor Mother! Ah, dear Mother!" On Good Friday, as we have said, oppressed by grief, and spiritually drowned in the bitterness of that great day, he could not even take food. Often he was heard to say, that Mary's greatest sorrow was when she saw her beloved Son dead in her arms, and saying this, he cried out, more by tears than words, with the affection of a truly loving heart, "Oh, grief above grief!" He himself related, in reference to this, that on one occasion, our Blessed Lady was seen in that most sorrowful act of receiving into her arms the lacerated Body of so dear a Son, and through her great sorrow and affliction, her face was like that of one dead. We do not know precisely who had this vision, but we find it deposed in the processes, that the servant of God, speaking one day with a priest, a dear friend of his, on the Passion of Jesus and the Dolours of Mary, drew from his sleeve, with a countenance all on fire, as was customary with him when he felt devotion, a little picture, representing Our Lady of Sorrows, drawn by Cavaliere Conca, who, being at the same time a skilful and excellent painter and a good Christian, painted it with great skill and devotion, at the request of the servant of God, who begged him to express her grief as strongly as he could, saying to him :—" Here, I give it to you because it is not sorrowful enough—I have seen her in greater sorrow;" and with these words gave him the holy picture, which is now preserved in the Monastery of Mount Carmel, at Vetralla. In the last years of his life, also, this most merciful Mother condescended to show herself to her faithful servant pierced with grief, as she was at the time of the most bitter passion of her dear Son; for in the retreat of Saints John and Paul, when after Mass he was making his thanksgiving in the room next the little chapel where he celebrated, she appeared to him with a sword through her heart, and tears in her eyes; and speaking of her Dolours, gave him so deep a sense of them, and used words of such tenderness, that they would even have rent a heart of stone. She gave him to understand that her sufferings were beyond measure, terrible, and overpowering, from the ardent love she bore to her Son, and the incomparable amplitude of her soul, capable of a sea of sorrows; the Queen of Sorrows complained of the false devotion of those who say they are devout to the Blessed Virgin, and then outrage by sin her Beloved Son; and with great force and tenderness exhorted her dear servant to promote, as he always did, devotion to the Sacred Passion of her Son, and to her Dolours. This Mother of Mercy, desiring to help a poor priest whose soul was in a wretched condition, manifested to Father Paul his necessities, and this priest having come into his presence afterwards, the servant of God, who saw his interior, said to him with a tone of certainty,

"You appear to me as ugly as a devil." At these words, the priest entering into himself, and acknowledging his dreadful state, prostrated himself in confusion and grief at the venerable Father's feet, promising to amend his life, and thus showed the truth of the apparition of Our Lady of Sorrows, who wished to draw him from the path of perdition. It is not, therefore, surprising that the servant of God, after such visions and so deep a perception of the Dolours of the Blessed Virgin, spoke of them with so much affection, tenderness, and compassion. As he knew what a treasure true devotion to our Blessed Lady is, he ardently desired that his children should enjoy the abundance of it. He inculcated, and with great fervour recommended, that they should be devout to our dear Lady. "Let them take," he says in the rules, "for their chief protectress, the ever Blessed Virgin Mary, Mother of God, and bear towards her a due devotion; let them often call to mind the most bitter sorrows endured by her during the Passion and

Death of her dear Son, and let them, by voice and example, promote in others devotion towards this great Lady."

COMMEMORATION OF THE SEVEN DOLOURS

OF THE

BLESSED VIRGIN MARY.

1.

Oh most afflicted of all Virgins! I feelingly commemorate the sorrow which filled thy most compassionate heart, when, on presenting thy Divine Son in the temple, holy Simeon foretold that a sword should pierce thy soul, thereby announcing the great share thou shouldst have in the sufferings of thy dear Son. I most devoutly compassionate thy grief on this occasion, and beseech thee, O Immaculate Queen of Martyrs, to obtain for me, through the Passion of Jesus Christ, which was the cause of all thy Dolours, a sincere and efficacious horror of sin, an ardent love of God, a practical devotion towards thee, and the grace of final perseverance.

Say one *Ave Maria* in honour of all the footsteps of Mary, for the grace of circumspection.

2.

Oh most afflicted and most guiltless of all the daughters of Eve! I feelingly commemorate the exceeding sorrow which filled thy maternal heart when thou didst see thy Divine Infant persecuted by his people, and wert obliged to flee into Egypt, in order to save Him from the fury of Herod. I most devoutly compassionate thy grief on that occasion, and beseech thee, O Immaculate Queen of Martyrs, to obtain for me, through the Passion of Jesus Christ, which was the cause of all thy Dolours, a sincere and efficacious horror of sin, an ardent love of God, a practical devotion towards thee, and the grace of a happy death.

Say one *Ave Maria* in honour of the lamentations of Mary, for the grace of compassion.

3.

Oh most sorrow-stricken Mother! I feelingly commemorate those rivers of sorrow which inundated thy maternal heart when thou wert separated from thy adorable Son, who remained for three days absent from thee after thy journey to Jerusalem. I most devoutly compassionate thy grief on that occasion, and beseech thee, O most gentle Queen of Martyrs, to obtain for me, through the Passion of Jesus Christ, which was the cause of thy Dolours, a sincere and efficacious horror of sin, an ardent love of God, a practical devotion towards thee, and the favour of thy assistance in my last agony.

Say one *Ave Maria* in honour of every sigh of agony which escaped from the sacred breast of Mary, for the grace of compassion for the poor and afflicted.

4.

Oh most afflicted Virgin! I feelingly commemorate the sorrow which filled thy maternal heart when thou didst follow thy dear Son to Mount Calvary, and beheldest Him sinking under the weight of the cross and of our sins. I most devoutly compassionate thy grief on that occasion, and beseech thee, O glorious Queen of Martyrs, to obtain for me, through the Passion of Jesus Christ, which was the cause of all thy Dolours, a sincere and efficacious horror of sin, an ardent love of God, a practical devotion towards thee, and a happy death under thy special protection.

Say one *Ave Maria* in honour of the tears of Mary, for the grace of Holy Purity.

5.

Oh most afflicted Virgin! I feelingly commemorate the sorrow which filled thy maternal heart when thou didst stand by the cross of Jesus, and didst witness all his torments, and see Him at length expire for the sins of the world. I devoutly compassionate thy grief on that occasion, O glorious Queen of Martyrs, and beseech thee to obtain for me, through the Passion of Jesus Christ, which was the cause of all thy Dolours, a sincere and efficacious horror of sin, an ardent love of God, a practical devotion towards thee, and a happy death under thy special protection.

Say one *Ave Maria* in honour of the afflicted heart of Mary, for the grace of Mercy.

6.

Oh most afflicted Virgin! I feelingly commemorate the sorrow which filled thy maternal heart when the adorable Body of thy Divine Son was taken down from the cross, and laid in thy arms. I most devoutly compassionate thy grief on that occasion, and beseech thee, O glorious Queen of Martyrs, to obtain for me, through the Passion of Jesus Christ, which was the cause of all thy Dolours, a sincere and efficacious horror of sin, an ardent love of God, a practical devotion towards thee, and a happy death under thy special protection.

Say one *Ave Maria* in honour of the

Sacred Arms of Mary, for that peace which the world cannot give.

7.

Oh most afflicted Virgin! I feelingly commemorate the sorrow which filled thy maternal heart, when the sacred Body of Jesus was taken from thy arms and laid in the holy sepulchre. I most devoutly compassionate thy grief on that occasion, and beseech thee, O glorious Queen of Martyrs, to obtain for me, through the Passion of Jesus Christ, which was the cause of all thy Dolours, a sincere and efficacious horror of sin, an ardent love of God, a practical devotion towards thee, and the grace of final perseverance.

Say one *Ave Maria* in honour of the sacred will of Mary, conformed to the will of Christ, for Holy Resignation.

LITANY OF OUR LADY OF SORROWS.*

Lord have mercy on us.
Christ have mercy on us.
Lord have mercy on us.
Christ hear us.
Christ graciously hear us.
God the Father of heaven,
God the Son, Redeemer of the world,
God the Holy Ghost,
Holy Trinity, one God,
Have mercy on us.

Holy Mary,
Holy Mother of God,
Holy Virgin of virgins,
Mother Crucified,
Mother most sorrowful,
Mother most tearful,
Mother most afflicted,
Mother most forsaken,
Mother most desolate,
Mother bereft of thy Child,
Pray for us.

---

* This Litany was written by Pius VII. in his captivity, who granted a plenary indulgence to all who recite it with a contrite heart, on Fridays.

Mother transfixed with the sword,
Mother consumed with grief,
Mother filled with anguish,
Mother crucified in heart,
Mother most sad,
Fountain of tears,
Mass of suffering,
Mirror of patience,
Rock of constancy,
Anchor of confidence,
Refuge of the forsaken,
Shield of the oppressed,
Subduer of the unbelieving,
Comfort of the wretched,
Medicine of the sick,
Strength of the weak,
Harbour of the wrecked,
Allayer of tempests,
Resource of mourners,
Terror of the treacherous,
Treasure of the faithful,
Eye of prophets,
Staff of apostles,
Crown of martyrs,
Light of confessors,
Pearl of virgins,
Consolation of widows,

Pray for us.

Lamb of God, who takest away the sins of the world,
Graciously hear us, O Jesus.
Lamb of God, who takest away the sins of the world,
Graciously hear us, O Jesus.
Lamb of God, who takest away the sins of the world,
Have mercy on us, O Jesus.

Look down upon us and deliver us from all trouble, in the power of Jesus Christ. Amen.

Imprint, O Lady, thy dolours upon my heart, that I may read therein sorrow and love: sorrow, to endure every sorrow for thee; love, to despise every love for thee.

Credo, Salve Regina, three *Ave Marias* in honour of *the Most Afflicted Heart of Mary.*

PRAYER.

O most afflicted Queen and Mother, by all thou didst endure during the three long hours Jesus hung upon the cross, but more especially by the bitter pangs which thou didst undergo at the moment of his death, I supplicate thee to engrave deeply on my heart his Wounds and thy Dolours; and when I come to die, prepare me by thy presence and prayers to pass from this world of sorrow to a happy eternity. Amen.

LAMENTATION OF MARY

AT THE
FOOT OF THE CROSS,
WITH
HER DEAD SON IN HER ARMS.

I.

Whilst Mary's arms her lifeless Son
  Close to her bosom press'd,
Deep drawn and bitter sighs broke out
  From her maternal breast;
Long did she view with tearful eyes
  His bleeding corse, and then
In broken accents thus bewail'd
  The cruelty of men.

II.

" Ah, me !" she said, " and can it be,
  I'll never more rejoice
To gaze upon thy beauteous smiles,
  Or hear thy tender voice;

Alas! how throbs my sinking breast
   To see Thee thus, my Son;
My heart must break, as thine has broke,
   For both hearts make but one.

III.

"Gone from thy lips are those sweet
   smiles
   That played around them once,
Gone from thy eyes that look of love
   That graced thy countenance;
I see thy face all bath'd in blood,
   That face whose looks could win
The hearts of all, and even hearts
   Long steep'd in loathsome sin.

IV.

"Those eyes once, like the stars of night,
   Shed lustre all around,
And even shone upon all those
   In sin's dark prison bound;
But now extinguished is their light,
   And with thy blood suffused,
Distorted by insulting blows,
   And, oh! so cruelly bruised.

V.

"Oh cruel lance! Oh scourges cruel!
  Oh torturing thorny crown!
Why thus combine my Son's fair form
  In his own Blood to drown?
He is the King of Heaven, yet
  His flesh you have illused,
Ah, see! His clotted Blood lies thick!
  See! all his limbs are bruised.

VI.

"And Thou art dead! Thou, whom I've
    nursed
  And kissed so many times;
Man! thou hast conquered, sinful man!
  And conquered by thy crimes;
Ah! ne'er shall I rejoice again,
  Nor seek to get relief,
My joy shall be in weeping,
  My only comfort—grief.

VII.

"But say, my martyred Jesus, say
  Whose sin has thus deserved
For Thee such cruel and bitter pangs;
  For Thee! th' Eternal Word.

Ah! I know well, my Jesus, yes—
  And all earth's creatures know,
It was the sins of guilty men
  That clothed Thee here below.

VIII.

"How strange to see the God of Love
  So spotless and so pure,
All these sad pains for others' sins
  Thus suffer and endure;
Oh power of hell! Oh power of sin!
  It seems that at thy nod,
The great and the immortal has
  Become a mortal God.

IX.

"O Father! look from heaven, look
  Upon thy murdered Child;
Cruel men his limbs have torn and cut;
  Yet He—so meek, so mild
So like a bruised rose he lies
  All crushed beneath their feet!
Yet mercy for all sinners
  Through the Sinless I entreat."

X.

Do thou, sweet Mother Mary,
   Trace thy Dolours on my heart,
And make me feel most keenly
   Compassion's piercing dart;
In thinking on thy sorrows,
   Let me pine away in grief,
Permit me not in creatures
   To seek to find relief. Amen.

Fathers and five Hail Marys in memory of the Passion.

II. Five years and as many quarantines, when members accompany the Blessed Sacrament to the sick.

III. Three hundred days once a day for those who say seven Hail Marys, followed by the verse Holy Mother, &c.

IV. One hundred and fifty days every time they meditate on the Passion or on the Dolours, and say seven Our Fathers and seven Hail Marys with the "Stabat Mater," or perform the spiritual exercises practised in the Churches of the Servites.

V. One hundred days for those who recite the "Stabat Mater."

VI. Sixty days for each work of Charity.

FEAST

OF THE

SEVEN DOLOURS OF THE BLESSED VIRGIN MARY.

Third Sunday in September.

VESPERS.

O quot undis lachrymarum.*

What a sea of tears and sorrow,
  Did the soul of Mary toss,
To and fro upon its billows,
  While she wept her bitter loss;
In her arms her Jesus holding,
  Torn but newly from the Cross!

O that mournful Virgin Mother,
  See her tears how fast they flow

---

* See *Lyra Catholica*.

Down upon his mangled body,
   Wounded side, and thorny brow,
While his hands and feet she kisses,—
   Picture of immortal woe!

Oft and oft his arms and bosom
   Fondly straining to her own;
Oft her pallid lips imprinting
   On each wound of her dear Son,
Till at last, in swoons of anguish,
   Sense and consciousness are gone.

Gentle Mother, we beseech thee,
   By thy tears and trouble sore,
By the death of thy dear Offspring,
   By the bloody wounds he bore,
Touch our hearts with that true sorrow,
   Which afflicted thee of yore.

To the Father everlasting,
   And the Son, who reigns on high,
With the co-eternal Spirit,
   Trinity in Unity,
Be salvation, honour, blessing,
   Now and through eternity.

MATINS.

Jam toto subditus vesper eat polo.

Come, darkness, spread o'er Heav'n thy
    pall,
  And hide, O sun, thy face,
While we that bitter death recall,
  With all its dire disgrace.

And thou, with tearful cheek, wast there,
  But with a heart of steel;
Mary, thou didst his moanings hear,
  And all his torments feel.

He hung before thee crucified,
  His flesh with scourgings rent,
His bloody gashes gaping wide,
  His strength and spirit spent.

Thou his dishonoured countenance
  And racking thirst didst see;
By turns the gall, the sponge, the lance,
  Were agony to thee.

Yet still erect in majesty
  Thou didst the sight sustain;

Oh more than martyr ! not to die
  Amid such cruel pain.

Praise to the blessed Three in One ;
  Oh may that strength be mine,
Which, sorrowing o'er her only Son,
  Did in the Virgin shine.

LAUDS.

Summæ Deus clementiæ.

God, in whom all grace doth dwell,
Grant us grace to ponder well
On the Virgin's Dolours seven,
On the wounds to Jesus given.

May the tears which Mary pour'd,
Gain us pardon of the Lord,
Tears sufficient in their worth
To wash out the guilt of earth.

May the contemplation sore
Of the five wounds Jesus bore,
Source to us of blessing be
Through a long eternity.

Glory be to Him who died,
For his servants, crucified,
Honour, praise, eternal merit
To the Father and the Spirit.

A NOVENA

IN HONOUR OF THE SEVEN DOLOURS.

From the Spanish.

Hail, O Sorrowful
Mother of Sorrows;
Mother of Sorrows,
Hail! Hail! Hail!

FIRST SORROW.

The Prophecy of Simeon.

Hail, fair Judith,
Who hast come to the temple
To receive the sword
Which is to pierce thee!
  Hail, O Sorrowful, &c.

PRAYER.

O most desolate of Mothers, seven most terrible swords of sorrow have penetrated thy soul! Each blow which Jesus received in this Passion reached thee; all His agonies depressed thy heart, but the last adieu He addressed to thee from the cross, reopened all thy former wounds and caused in thee greater suffering than all God's creatures have ever felt in dying. O Mother of grief and of love, I come to intreat thy intercession, convinced of my own unworthiness to obtain thy favours, and beseeching thee in the name of Jesus and through thy love for His Sacred Heart in the Divine Sacrament, to obtain for me the intentions of this Novena. Remember, most holy Queen of Martyrs, that thy honour is concerned therein, and that St. Bernard, says, "that no one ever asked thee in vain." Hail, Mary, &c.

O Mary, Mother of Dolours, conceived without sin, pray for us who have recourse to thee.

SECOND SORROW.

The Flight into Egypt.

Hail, beautiful Sara,
Who camest to Egypt,
Fleeing from Herod,
And there didst take shelter.
   Hail, O Sorrowful, &c.
 Prayer, Hail Mary, &c.

THIRD SORROW.

The Child Lost.

Hail, turtle-dove;
Three days wandering
Thou seekest, lamenting,
Thy tender Infant!
   Hail, O Sorrowful, &c.
 Prayer, Hail Mary, &c.

FOURTH SORROW.

The Bearing of the Cross.

Hail, weeping Hagar,
Thou runnest along the valley,

The roads and the squares
To the street of Bitterness!
    Hail, O Sorrowful, &c.
Prayer, Hail Mary, &c.

FIFTH SORROW.

Jesus Christ is Crucified.

Hail, Sea of Bitterness,
Rock impenetrable
To the nail and the hammer,
The lance and the cross so dear!
    Hail, O Sorrowful, &c.
Prayer, Hail Mary, &c.

SIXTH SORROW.

The Anguish.

Hail, O moon, full
Of anguish and ills,
Torments and pains,
And exceeding outrages!
    Hail, O Sorrowful, &c.,
Prayer, Hail Mary, &c.

SEVENTH SORROW.

The Loneliness.

Hail, lonely Queen
Of troubles;
Noemi, the most lonely
That ever lived.
   Hail, O Sorrowful, &c.
 Prayer, Hail Mary, &c.

Hail, Mother of the Machabees,
Seven times martyr,
May thy seven sorrows
Protect and defend us.
   Hail, O Sorrowful, &c.

Blessed and praised be
The most Holy Trinity
And the Most Holy Sacrament
Of the Altar.
Incarnate without injury
To that virginal womb
Of Mary, conceived
Without original sin,
From the very first moment
Of her existence. Amen, Jesu!

"Vouchsafe, O Mother of Sorrows, conceived without sin, to imprint all the wounds of thy Crucified Son and all thy Dolours deeply on my heart."

By reciting seven Hail Marys, and the above aspiration after each, with a contrite heart, Pope Pius VII. granted 300 day's Indulgence, and a Plenary Indulgence once a month if said daily for a month, by approaching the Sacraments, and praying for the intentions of the Church.

NOTE.—Confession to be made, and the Most Holy Communion approached once during the nine days, and both to be offered for the intentions of the Novena.

MASS OF THE SEVEN DOLOURS

OF THE

BLESSED VIRGIN MARY,

FOR THE THIRD SUNDAY IN SEPTEMBER AND

FOR THE FRIDAY IN PASSION WEEK.

Placing thyself, dear Christian soul, in spirit with Mary the Queen of Martyrs at the foot of the Cross of Jesus Crucified, offer to his Sacred Heart the adorable Sacrifice of the Mass, in honour of the Seven Dolours, for thy own wants, the intentions of the Church, and for the ends for which Jesus died. Then, making acts of Faith, Hope, and Charity, begin with the priest as follows:—

In nomine Patris, et Filii, et Spiritus	In the name of the Father, and of the

Sancti. Amen.

P. Introibo ad altare Dei.

R. Ad Deum qui lætificat juventutem meam.

Son, and of the Holy Ghost. Amen.

P. I will go into the altar of God.

R. To God who giveth joy to my youth.

Psalm xlii.

P. Judica me, Deus, et discerne causam meam de gente non sancta: ab homine iniquo et doloso erue me.

R. Quia tu es, Deus, fortitudo mea: quare me repulisti, et quare tristis incedo dum affligit me inimicus?

P. Emitte lucem tuam et veritatem tuam: ipsa me deduxerunt et adduxerunt in

P. Judge me, O God, and distinguish my cause from the nation that is not holy: deliver me from the unjust and deceitful man.

R. For thou art, God, my strength; why hast thou cast me off? and why go I sorrowful whilst the enemy afflicteth me?

P. Send forth thy light and thy truth: they have conducted me and brought me unto thy holy hill

montem sanctum tuum, et in tabernacula tua.

R. Et introibo ad altare Dei: ad Deum qui lætificat juventutem meam.

P. Confitebor tibi in cithara, Deus, Deus meus: quare tristis es, anima mea? et quare conturbas me?

R. Spera in Deo, quoniam adhuc confitebor illi: salutare vultus mei, et Deus meus.

P. Gloria Patri, et Filio et Spiritui Sancto.

R. Sicut erat in principio, et nunc

and into thy tabernacles.

R. And I will go unto the altar of God: to God who giveth joy to my youth.

P. To thee, O God, my God, I will give praise upon the harp: why art thou sad, O my soul, and why dost thou disquiet me?

R. Hope in God, for I will still give praise to Him, the salvation of my countenance and my God.

P. Glory be to the Father, and to the Son, and to the Holy Ghost.

R. As it was in the beginning is

et semper et in sæcula sæculorum. Amen.

P. Introibo ad altare Dei.

R. Ad Deum qui lætificat juventutem meam.

P. Adjutorium nostrum in nomine Domini.

R. Qui fecit cœlum et terram.

P. Confiteor Deo omnipotenti, beatæ Mariæ semper Virgini, beato Joanni Baptistæ, sanctis Apostolis Petro et Paulo, omnibus Sanctis et vobis, fratres, quia peccavi nimis cogitatione, verbo, et opere; mea culpa, mea culpa, mea maxima culpa. Ideo precor

now and ever shall be, world without end. Amen.

P. I will go into the altar of God.

R. To God who giveth joy to my youth.

P. Our help is in the name of the Lord.

R. Who made heaven and earth.

P. I confess to Almighty God, to blessed Mary, ever Virgin, to blessed Michael the Archangel, to blessed John the Baptist, to the holy Apostles Peter and Paul, to all the Saints, and to you, brethren, that I have sinned exceedingly, in thought, word, and

beatam Mariam semper Virginem, beatum Michaelem Archangelum, beatum Joannem Baptistam, sanctos Apostolos Petrum et Paulum, omnes Sanctos, et vos, fratres, orare pro me ad Dominum Deum nostrum.

deed; through my fault, through my fault, through my most grievous fault. Therefore I beseech the blessed Mary, ever Virgin, blessed Michael the Archangel, blessed John the Baptist, the holy Apostles Peter and Paul, all the Saints, and you, brethren, to pray to the Lord our God for me.

R. Misereatur tui omnipotens Deus, et dimissis peccatis tuis, perducat te ad vitam æternam.

R. May Almighty God be merciful to thee, and thy sins being forgiven, bring thee to everlasting life.

P. Amen.

P. Amen.

R. Confiteor Deo, etc.

R. I confess, etc.

P. Misereatur vestri omnipotens Deus, et dimissis

P. May Almighty God be merciful to you, and your sins

peccatis vestris, perducat vos ad vitam æternam.

R. Amen.

P. ✠ Indulgentiam, absolutionem, et remissionem peccatorum nostrorum tribuat nobis omnipotens et misericors Dominus.

R. Amen.

P. Deus, tu conversus vivificabis nos.

R. Et plebs tua lætabitur in te.

P. Ostende nobis, Domine, misericordiam tuam.

R. Et salutare tuum da nobis.

P. Domine, exaudi orationem meam.

being forgiven, bring you to everlasting life.

R. Amen.

P. ✠ May the Almighty and merciful God grant us pardon, absolution, and remission of our sins.

R. Amen.

P. O God, thou being turned towards us, wilt enliven us.

R. And thy people will rejoice in thee.

P. Show us, O Lord, thy mercy.

R. And grant us thy salvation.

P. O Lord, hear my prayer.

R. Et clamor meus ad te veniat.
R. And let my cry come unto thee.

P. Dominus vobiscum.
P. The Lord be with you.

R. Et cum spiritu tuo.
R. And with thy spirit.

P. Oremus.
P. Let us pray.

The Priest going up to the Altar, says:—

Aufer a nobis, quæsumus, Domine, iniquitates nostras; ut ad Sancta Sanctorum puris mereamur mentibus introire. Per Christum Dominum nostrum. Amen.
Take away from us, we beseech thee, O Lord, our iniquities, that we may deserve to enter into the Holy of Holies with pure minds. Through Christ our Lord. Amen.

When the Priest arrives at the Altar, bowing down, he says:—

Oramus te, Domine, per merita sanctorum tuorum quorum reliquiæ
We beseech thee, O Lord, by the merit of those saints whose relics are here, and

hic sunt, et omnium of all the saints, to sanctorum ut indulgere digneris all my sins. Amen. omnia peccata mea. Amen.

Here, at Solemn High Mass, the Priest blesses incense by the sign of the cross, saying these words:—

Ab illo benedicaris, in cujus honore cremaberis. Amen.

Mayest thou be blessed by him in whose honour thou shalt be burnt. Amen.

And then incenses the altar, after which he turns to the book and reads the Introit : St. John xix.

Stabant juxta crucem Jesu mater ejus et soror matris ejus, Maria Cleophæ et Salome, et Maria Magdalena. Mulier, ecce filius tuus, dixit Jesus : ad discipulum au-

There stood by the cross of Jesus his mother and his mother's sister, Mary of Cleophas and Salome, and Mary Magdalen. Woman, behold thy Son, said Jesus ; to

tem ; ecce Mater tua. Gloria Patri et Filio et Spiritui Sancto: sicut erat in principio et nunc et semper et in sæcula sæculorum. Amen. Stabant juxta crucem etc.

his disciple, however; Behold thy mother. Glory be to the Father, and to the Son, and to the Holy Ghost: as it was in the beginning is now and ever shall be, world without end. Amen.

Returning to the middle of the altar, he says:—

P. Kyrie eleison.   P. Lord have mercy on us.
R. Kyrie eleison.   R. Lord have mercy on us.
P. Kyrie eleison.   P. Lord have mercy on us.
R. Christe eleison. R. Christ have mercy on us.
P. Christe eleison. P. Christ have mercy on us.
R. Christe eleison. R. Christ have mercy on us.
P. Kyrie eleison.   P. Lord have mercy on us.

R. Kyrie eleison.   R. Lord have mercy on us.

P. Kyrie eleison.   P. Lord have mercy on us.

Gloria in excelsis Deo; et in terra pax hominibus bonæ voluntatis. Laudamus te; benedicimus te; adoramus te; glorificamus te. Gratias agimus tibi propter magnam gloriam tuam. Domine Deus, Rex cælestis, Deus Pater omnipotens. Domine Fili unigenite, Jesu Christe: Domine Deus, Agnus Dei, Filius Patris, qui tollis peccata mundi, miserere nobis: qui tollis peccata mundi, suscipe de-

Glory be to God on high, and on earth peace to men of good will. We praise Thee, we bless Thee, we adore Thee, we glorify Thee. We give Thee thanks for thy great glory. O Lord God, heavenly King, God the Father Almighty. O Lord Jesus Christ, the only begotten Son: O Lord God, Lamb of God, Son of the Father, who takest away the sins of the world, have mercy on us: thou who takest away the sins of the world,

precationem nostram : qui sedes ad dexteram Patris, miserere nobis. Quoniam tu solus sanctus : tu solus Dominus : tu solus altissimus, Jesu Christe, cum Sancto Spiritu, in gloria Dei Patris. Amen.

receive our prayers: Thou who sittest at the right hand of the Father, have mercy on us. For Thou only art holy : Thou only art the Lord : Thou only, O Jesus Christ, with the Holy Ghost, art most high, in the glory of God the Father. Amen.

He kisses the altar, and turning to the people, says:—

P. Dominus vobiscum.

P. The Lord be with you.

R. Et cum spiritu tuo.

R. And with thy spirit.

P. Oremus.

P. Let us pray.

PRAYER.

Deus, in cujus passione secundum Simeonis prophetiam, dulcissimam animam gloriosæ

O God, in whose Passion, according to the prophecy of Simeon, a sword of sorrow pierced the

Virginis et Matris Mariæ, doloris gladius pertransivit; concede propitius; ut qui transfixionem ejus et passionem venerando recolimus, gloriosis meritis et precibus omnium sanctorum cruci fideliter astantium intercedentibus, passionis tuæ effectum felicem consequamur. Qui vivis, &c.

In Missis Votivis dicatur sequens Oratio.

most sweet soul of the glorious Mary, Mother and Virgin; grant in thy mercy that we who call to mind with veneration her transfixion and sufferings, by the glorious merits and prayers of the saints faithfully standing by the cross interceding for us, may obtain the happy effect of thy Passion.

The following prayer is said instead in votive Masses:—

Interveniat pro nobis, quæsumus, Domine Jesu Christe, nunc, et in hora mortis nostræ, apud tuam clementiam beata

Grant, we beseech thee, O Lord Jesus Christ, that the Blessed Virgin thy Mother may intercede for us with thy clemency now and at

Virgo Maria mater tua; cujus sacratissimam animam in hora passionis tuæ doloris gladius pertransivit. Qui vivis, etc.

the hour of our death, who in the hour of thy Passion was pierced in her most holy soul by a sword of sorrow. Grant this, O Jesus Christ, etc.

Lectio libri Judith:

Lesson:

Judith xiii.

Judith xiii, 22-25.

Benedixit te Dominus in virtute sua, quia per te ad nihilum redegit inimicos nostros. Benedicta es tu, filia, a Domino Deo excelso, prae omnibus mulieribus super terram. Benedictus Dominus, qui creavit coelum et terram: quia hodie nomen tuum ita magnifi-

The Lord hath blessed thee by his power, who by thee hath brought our enemies to nought. Blessed art thou, O Daughter, by the Lord, the Most High God, above all women upon earth. Blessed be the Lord, who made heaven and earth, because he hath so magnified thy name this day,

cavit, ut non recedat laus tua de ore hominum, qui memores fuerint virtutis Domini in æternum, pro quibus non pepercisti animæ tuæ propter angustias et tribulationem generis tui, sed subvenisti ruinæ ante conspectum Dei nostri. Deo Gratias.

that thy praise shall not depart out of the mouth of men who shall be mindful of the power of the Lord for ever; for that thou hast not spared thy life, by reason of the distress and tribulation of thy people, but hast prevented our ruin in the presence of our Lord. Thanks be to God.

Graduale. Dolorosa, et lacrymabilis es, Virgo Maria, stans juxta crucem Domini Jesu Filii tui Redemptoris.

V. Virgo Dei Genitrix, quem totus non capit orbis, hoc Crucis fert sup-

Gradual. Thou art all sorrowful, and full of tears, O Virgin Mary, standing near the Cross of the Lord Jesus Christ, thy Son, and our Redeemer; O Virgin Mother of God, He whom the whole

plicium vitæ, factus homo.

Alleluja, Alleluja.

V. Stabat Sancta cœli Regina, et mundi Domina juxta Crucem Domini nostri Jesu Christi dolorosa. Alleluja.

Post Septuagesimam, omissa Alleluja, dicatur: Stabat, etc.

Tunc: O vos omnes, qui transitis per viam, attendite, et videte, si est dolor sicut dolor meus.

Tempore Paschali, Alleluja, Alleluja. Tunc: Stabat, etc., Alleluja. Deinde, O vos omnes, etc. Alleluja.

world doth not contain, beareth this punishment of the Cross of life, being made man.

Alleluja, Alleluja.

V. Holy Mary, the Queen of Heaven and Mistress of the World, stood by the Cross of our Lord Jesus Christ, full of sadness. Alleluja.

After Septuagesima Sunday, the Allelujas are omitted, and Holy Mary, etc., is said, together with the following:

"O all ye that pass by the way, attend and see if there be any sorrow like my sorrow."

Stabat Mater.

Stabat Mater dolorosa
   Juxta crucem lacrymosa
   Dum pendebat Filius.
Cujus animam gementem,
   Contristatam et dolentem,
   Pertransivit gladius.

O quam tristis et afflicta
   Fuit illa benedicta
   Mater Unigeniti!
Quæ mœrebat, et dolebat,
   Pia Mater dum videbat
   Nati pœnas inclyti.

Quis est homo qui non fleret,
   Matrem Christi si videret
   In tanto supplicio?
Quis non posset contristari
   Christi Matrem contemplari
   Dolentem cum Filio?

Pro peccatis suæ gentis
   Vidit Jesum in tormentis,
   Et flagellis subditum.

Stabat Mater.

At the Cross her station keeping,
Stood the mournful Mother weeping,
   Close to Jesus to the last:
Through her heart, his sorrows sharing,
All his bitter anguish bearing,
   Now at length the sword had passed.

Oh, how sad and sore distressed
Was that Mother, highly blest,
   Of the sole-begotten One!
Christ above in torment hangs;
She beneath beholds the pangs
   Of her dying glorious Son.

Is there one who would not weep,
'Whelmed in miseries so deep,
   Christ's dear Mother to behold?
Can the human heart refrain
From partaking in her pain,
   In that Mother's pain untold?

Bruised, derided, cursed, defiled,
She beheld her tender Child,
   All with bloody scourges rent;

Vidit suum dulcem natum
 Moriendo desolatum
 Dum emisit Spiritum.

Eja Mater, fons amoris,
 Me sentire vim doloris
 Fac, ut tecum lugeam :
Fac ut ardeat cor meum
 In amando Christum Deum,
 Ut sibi complaceam.

Sancta Mater, istud agas,
 Crucifixi fige plagas
 Cordi meo valide.
Tui Nati vulnerati,
 Tam dignati pro me pati,
 Pœnas mecum divide.

Fac me tecum pie flere,
 Crucifixo condolere,
 Donec ego vixero.
Juxta crucem tecum stare,
 Et me tibi sociare
 In planctu desidero.

Virgo Virginum præclara,
 Mihi jam non sis amara,

For the sins of his own nation,
Saw Him hang in desolation
   Till his Spirit forth he sent.

O thou Mother! Fount of love!
Touch my spirit from above,
   Make my heart with thine accord:
Make me feel as thou hast felt;
Make my soul to glow and melt
   With the love of Christ my Lord.

Holy Mother! pierce me through;
In my heart each wound renew
   Of my Saviour crucified;
Let me share with thee his pain,
Who for all my sins was slain,
   Who for me in torments died.

Let me mingle tears with thee,
Mourning Him who mourned for me,
   All the days that I may live:
By the Cross with thee to stay,
There with thee to weep and pray,
   Is all I ask of thee to give.

Virgin of all virgins best!
Listen to my fond request:

Fac me tecum plangere.
Fac, ut portem Christi mortem,
Passionis fac consortem,
Et plagas recolere.

Fac me plagis vulnerari,
Fac me Cruce inebriari,
Et cruore Filii.
Flammis ne urar succensus,
Per te, Virgo, sim defensus
In die judicii.

Christe, cum sit hinc exire,
Da per Matrem me venire
Ad palmam victoriæ.
Quando corpus morietur,
Fac ut animæ donetur
Paradisi gloria. Amen.*

Munda cor meum ac labia mea, Omnipotens Deus, qui labia Isaiæ Prophetæ calculo mundasti ignito: ita me tua grata miseratione dignare mundare, ut sanctum Evangelium tuum digne valeam nuntiare. Per Christum Dominum nostrum. Amen.

---

* An Indulgence of 100 days to all the faithful every time that in honour of the Sorrows of the B.V Mary they devoutly recite the Stabat Mater.

Let me share thy grief divine;
Let me to my latest breath,
In my body bear the death
Of that dying Son of thine.

Wounded with his every wound,
Steep my soul till it hath swooned
In his very Blood away;
Be to me, O Virgin, nigh,
Lest in flames I burn and die
In his awful judgment-day.

Christ, when thou shalt call me hence,
Be thy Mother my defence,
Be thy Cross my victory:
While my body here decays,
May my soul thy goodness praise
Safe in Paradise with Thee. Amen.

Cleanse my heart and my lips, O Almighty God, who didst cleanse the lips of the Prophet Isaias with a burning coal; vouchsafe so to cleanse me by thy gracious mercy that I may be able worthily to proclaim thy holy Gospel. Through Jesus Christ our Lord. Amen.

Jube, Domine, benedicere.

Dominus sit in corde meo et in labiis meis ut digne et competenter annuntiem Evangelium suum. Amen.

P. Dominus vobiscum.

R. Et cum spiritu tuo.

P. Sequentia sancti Evangelii secundum Joannem. C. 19.

R. Gloria tibi, Domine.

In illo tempore: Stabant juxta crucem Jesu mater ejus et soror matris ejus Maria Cleophæ et Maria Magdalena. Cum vidisset ergo Jesus

Give me thy blessing, Father.

May the Lord be in my heart, and on my lips, that I may worthily and in a proper manner announce his Gospel. Amen.

P. The Lord be with you.

R. And with thy spirit.

P. Continuation of the holy Gospel according to John. C. 19.

R. Glory be to Thee, O Lord.

Gospel. At that time there stood by the cross of Jesus his mother, and his mother's sister, Mary of Cleophas, and Mary Magdalen. When Jesus,

matrem, et discipulum stantem quem diligebat, dicit matri suæ: Mulier, ecce filius tuus. Deinde dicit discipulo: Ecce mater tua. Et ex illa hora accepit eam discipulus in sua.

therefore, had seen his mother and the disciple standing, whom he loved, he saith to his mother: Woman behold thy son. After that he saith to his disciple: Behold thy mother. And from that hour the disciple took her to his own.

R. Laus tibi, Christe.

R. Praise to Thee, O Christ.

The priest kisses the book, saying:—

Per Evangelica dicta deleantur nostra delicta.

By the words of the Gospel may our sins be blotted out.

Then the priest, at the middle of the altar, says the Nicene Creed (when appointed to be said) as follows:—

Credo in unum Deum, Patrem omnipotentem, factorem cœli et terræ,

I believe in one God, the Father Almighty, maker of heaven and earth,

visibilium omnium et invisibilium.	and of all things visible and invisible.
Et in unum Dominum Jesum Christum Filium Dei Unigenitum, et ex Patre natum ante omnia sæcula. Deum de Deo, Lumen de Lumine, Deum verum de Deo vero, genitum non factum, consubstantialem Patri, per quem omnia facta sunt. Qui propter nos homines, et propter nostram salutem, descendit de cœlis, et incarnatus est de Spiritu Sancto, ex Maria Virgine. *Et Homo Factus Est.* Crucifixus etiam pro nobis, sub Pontio Pilato,	And in one Lord Jesus Christ, the only-begotten Son of God, born of the Father before all ages. God of God, Light of Light, true God of true God, begotten not made, consubstantial with the Father, by whom all things were made. Who for us men, and for our salvation, came down from heaven and was incarnate by the Holy Ghost of the Virgin Mary. *And was made man.* He was crucified also for us, suffered under Pontius Pilate, and was buried. The third

passus et sepultus est. Et resurrexit tertia die secundum Scripturas, et ascendit in cœlum, sedet ad dexteram Patris, et iterum venturus est cum gloria judicare vivos et mortuos: cujus regni non erit finis.

Et in Spiritum Sanctum, Dominum et vivificantem, qui ex Patre Filioque procedit, qui cum Patre et Filio simul adoratur et conglorificatur, qui locutus est per prophetas. Et unam sanctam Catholicam et Apostolicam Ecclesiam. Confiteor unum baptisma in

day he rose again, according to the Scriptures, and ascended into heaven, and sitteth at the right hand of the Father, and he shall come again with glory to judge the living and the dead: of whose kingdom there shall be no end.

And I believe in the Holy Ghost, the Lord and life-giver, who proceedeth from the Father and the Son, who, together with the Father and the Son, is adored and glorified, who spake by the prophets. And one holy, Catholic, and Apostolic Church. I confess one baptism for the remission

remissionem peccatorum. Et expecto resurrectionem mortuorum, et vitam venturi sæculi. Amen.

of sins. And I expect the resurrection of the dead, and the life of the world to come. Amen.

He kisses the altar, and turning to the people, says:—

P. Dominus vobiscum.

P. The Lord be with you.

R. Et cum spiritu tuo.

R. And with thy spirit.

Reading the Offertory, he says:—

Offertorium. Recordare, Virgo Mater Dei, dum steteris in conspectu Domini, ut loquaris pro nobis bona, et ut avertat indignationem suam a nobis.

Be mindful, O Virgin Mother of God, when thou standest in the sight of the Lord to speak good things for us, that He may turn away his wrath from us.

Then taking the paten with the Host, he continues as follows:—

Suscipe, sancte

Receive, O Holy

Pater, omnipotens, æterne Deus, hanc immaculatam Hostiam, quam ego indignus famulus tuus offero tibi, Deo meo vivo et vero, pro innumerabilibus peccatis, offensionibus, et negligentiis meis, et pro omnibus circumstantibus, sed et pro omnibus fidelibus Christianis, vivis atque defunctis, ut mihi et illis proficiat ad salutem in vitam æternam. Amen.

Father Almighty, eternal God, this immaculate Host, which I, thy unworthy servant, offer unto thee, my living and true God, for my innumerable sins, offences, and negligences, and for all here present, as also for all faithful Christians, both living and dead, that it may be profitable for my own and for their salvation unto life eternal. Amen.

Putting wine and water into the chalice, he says:—

Deus, ✠ qui humanæ substantiæ dignitatem mira-

Oh God, who didst wonderfully constitute the dig-

biliter condidisti, et mirabilius reformasti; da nobis per hujus aquæ et vini mysterium ejus divinitatis esse consortes, qui humanitatis nostræ fieri dignatus est particeps, Jesus Christus, Filius tuus, Dominus noster; qui tecum vivit et regnat in unitate Spiritus Sancti Deus, per omnia sæcula sæculorum. Amen.

nity of human nature, and still more wonderfully reform it; grant that by the mystery of this water and wine, we may be partakers of his Divinity, who vouchsafed to become a partaker of our human nature, Jesus Christ, thy Son, our Lord, who liveth and reigneth with Thee, in the unity of the Holy Ghost, world without end. Amen.

Offering up the chalice, he says:—

Offerimus tibi, Domine, calicem salutaris, tuam deprecantes clementiam, ut in conspectu divinæ Majestatis tuæ, pro-

We offer to Thee, O Lord, the chalice of salvation, beseeching thy clemency, that it ascend with an odour of sweetness in the

nostra et totius mundi salute cum odore suavitatis ascendat. Amen.

sight of thy divine Majesty, for our salvation, and that of the whole world. Amen.

Bowing down before the altar, he says:—

In spiritu humilitatis, et in animo contrito, suscipiamur a te, Domine, et sic fiat sacrificium nostrum in conspectu tuo hodie, ut placeat tibi, Domine Deus.

May we be received by Thee, O, Lord, in the spirit of humility, and in a contrite mind; and so may our sacrifice be made in thy sight this day, that it may be pleasing to Thee, O Lord God.

Raising his hands and eyes, he says:—

Veni, sanctificator, omnipotens æterne Deus, et benedic hoc sacrificium, tuo sancto nomini præparatum.

Come, O Almighty and eternal God, the sanctifier, and bless this sacrifice prepared for thy holy name.

At High Mass he blesses the incense, saying :—

Per intercessionem beati Michaelis Archangeli, stantis a dextris Altaris Incensi, et omnium electorum suorum, incensum istud dignetur Dominus benedicere, et in odorem suavitatis accipere. Per Christum Dominum nostrum. Amen.

By the intercession of blessed Michael the archangel, standing on the right hand of the Altar of Incense, and of all his elect, may the Lord vouchsafe to bless this incense, and receive it as an odour of sweetness, through Christ our Lord. Amen.

The Priest incenses the bread and wine, saying :—

Incensum istud a te benedictum ascendat ad te, Domine, et descendat super nos misericordia tua.

May this incense blessed by Thee, ascend to Thee, O Lord, and may thy mercy descend upon us.

Then he incenses the altar, saying :—

Dirigatur, Domine, oratio mea sicut incensum in conspectu tuo; elevatio manuum mearum sacrificium vespertinum. Pone, Domine, custodiam ori meo et ostium circumstantiæ labiis meis, ut non declinet cor meum in verba malitiæ ad excusandas excusationes in peccatis.	Let my prayer be directed, O Lord, as incense in thy sight; the lifting up of my hands as evening sacrifice. Set a watch, O Lord, before my mouth, and a door round about my lips, that my heart may not incline to evil words to make excuses in sins.

Returning the thurible to the Deacon, he says:—

Accendat in nobis Dominus ignem sui amoris et flammam æternæ caritatis. Amen.	May the Lord enkindle within us the fire of his love, and the flame of eternal charity. Amen.

Washing his hands, he says:—

Lavabo inter innocentes manus	I will wash my hands among the

meas; et circumdabo altare tuum, Domine.

Ut audiam vocem laudis et enarrem universa mirabilia tua.

Domine, dilexi decorem domus tuæ, et locum habitationis gloriæ tuæ.

Ne perdas cum impiis, Deus, animam meam; et cum viris sanguinum vitam meam.

In quorum manibus iniquitates sunt; dextra eorum repleta est muneribus.

Ego autem in innocentia mea ingressus sum; redime me, et miserere mei.

innocent, and will compass thy altar, O Lord.

That I may hear the voice of praise, and tell of all thy marvellous works.

O Lord, I have loved the beauty of thy house, and the place where thy glory dwelleth.

Take not away my soul, O God, with the wicked; nor my life with bloody men.

In whose hands are iniquities, their right hand is filled with gifts.

But as for me, I have walked in my innocence; redeem me and have mercy on me.

Pes meus stetit in directo; in ecclesiis benedicam te Domine.

Gloria Patri, etc.

Suscipe, Sancta Trinitas, hanc oblationem quam tibi offerimus ob memoriam Passionis, Resurrectionis, et Ascensionis Jesu Christi Domini nostri: et in honorem Beatæ Mariæ semper Virginis, et beati Joannis Baptistæ, et sanctorum Apostolorum Petri et Pauli, et istorum et omnium Sanctorum: ut illis proficiat ad honorem,

My foot hath stood in the direct way; in the churches I will bless Thee, O Lord.

Glory be to the Father, etc.

Receive, O Holy Trinity, this oblation, which we offer to Thee in memory of the Passion, Resurrection, and Ascension of our Lord Jesus Christ, and in honour of the Blessed Virgin Mary, and blessed John Baptist, and the holy Apostles Peter and Paul, and of these and of all the Saints; that it may be to their honour and our salvation: and may

nobis autem ad salutem: et illi pro nobis intercedere dignentur in cœlis, quorum memoriam agimus in terris. Per eundem Christum Dominum nostrum. Amen.	they vouchsafe to intercede for us in Heaven, whose memory we celebrate on earth. Through Christ our Lord. Amen.

Turning to the people, he says aloud :—

Orate, fratres,	Brethren, pray,

And continues in a low voice,

Ut meum ac vestrum sacrificium acceptabile fiat apud Deum Patrem omnipotentem.	That my sacrifice and yours may be acceptable to God the Father Almighty.

The Acolyte answers :—

Suscipiat Dominus sacrificium de manibus tuis, ad laudem et gloriam nominis sui, ad	May the Lord receive the sacrifice from thy hands, to the praise and glory of his name, for our

utilitatem quoque nostram, totiusque Ecclesiæ suæ sanctæ.

benefit, and that of all his holy Church.

Then he reads :—

Secreta.

Offerimus tibi preces et hostias, Domine Jesu Christe, humiliter supplicantes : ut, qui Transfixionem dulcissimi spiritus Beatæ Mariæ matris tuæ precibus recensemus : suae suorumque sub cruce sanctorum consortium multiplicato piissimo interventu, meritis mortis tuae, meritum cum beatis habeamus. Qui vivis, etc.

The Secret.

We offer Thee, O Lord Jesus Christ, our prayers and sacrifices, humbly intreating Thee, that we, who, in our prayers of this day commemorate the Transfixion of the most sweet soul of Blessed Mary, thy Mother, may receive our reward with her and her faithful companions that stood under thy Cross, this holy assembly being multiplied through the merits of thy death. Who livest, etc.

P. Per omnia sæcula sæculorum.
R. Amen.
P. Dominus vobiscum.
R. Et cum spiritu tuo.
P. Sursum corda.
R. Habemus ad Dominum.
P. Gratias agamus Domino Deo nostro.
R. Dignum et justum est.
Vere dignum et justum est, æquum et salutare nos tibi semper et ubique gratias agere et te in Transfixione Beatæ Mariæ semper Virginis collaudare, benedicere, et prædicare.

P. World without end.
R. Amen.
P. The Lord be with you.
R. And with thy spirit.
P. Raise up your hearts.
R. We have raised them up to the Lord.
P. Let us give thanks to the Lord our God.
R. It is meet and just.
It is truly meet and just, right and available to salvation, that we should everywhere and at all times thank Thee, O Lord, but especially that we should praise, bless and extol Thee on the Transfixion of

Quæ et Unigenitum tuum Sancti Spiritus obumbratione concepit, et virginitatis gloria permanente, lumen æternum mundo effudit Jesum Christum Dominum nostrum: per quem Majestatem tuam laudant angeli, adorant dominationes, tremunt potestates, cœli cœlorumque virtutes, ac beata seraphim, socia exultatione concelebrant. Cum quibus et nostras voces ut admitti jubeas deprecamur, supplici confessione dicentes :	Blessed Mary ever Virgin, who both conceived thy only begotten Son, by the overshadowing of the Holy Ghost, and, without losing the glory of Virginity, brought forth to the world the Eternal Light, Jesus Christ our Lord; through whom the angels praise thy Majesty, the dominations adore, the powers tremble. The heavens and the powers of the heavens, and the blessed seraphim celebrate it together with equal exultation. With whom we beg that thou wouldst com-

	mand our voices also to be admitted, saying, with suppliant confession:
Sanctus, sanctus, sanctus,	Holy, Holy, Holy,
Dominus, Deus Sabaoth:	Lord God of Hosts:
Pleni sunt cœli et terra gloria tua.	The heavens and earth are full of thy glory.
Hosanna in excelsis.	Hosanna in the highest.
Benedictus qui venit in nomine Domini.	Blessed is he that cometh in the name of the Lord.
Hosanna in excelsis.	Hosanna in the highest.

THE CANON OF THE MASS.

The Priest says in a low voice:—

Te igitur, clementissime Pater, per Jesum Christum Filium tuum Dominum nostrum, supplices rogamus ac peti-	We humbly beg and beseech Thee, therefore, O most merciful Father, through Jesus Christ thy Son our Lord, to accept and

mus, uti accepta habeas et benedicas hæc ✠ dona, hæc ✠ munera, hæc ✠ sancta sacrificia illibata, in primis, quæ tibi offerimus pro Ecclesia tua sancta Catholica, quam pacificare, custodire, adunare, et regere digneris toto orbe terrarum, una cum famulo tuo Papa nostro N. et Antistite nostro N. et omnibus orthodoxis atque Catholicæ et Apostolicæ Fidei cultoribus.

bless these gifts, these presents, these holy undefiled sacrifices which we offer Thee, especially for thy Holy Catholic Church; which vouchsafe to pacify, preserve, unite, and govern, throughout the world, together with thy servant our Pope N. and our Bishop N., and all orthodox persons and professors of the Catholic and Apostolic faith.

COMMEMORATION OF THE LIVING.

Memento, Domine, famulorum

Remember, O Lord, thy servants

famularumque of both sexes, N. tuarum, N. et N. and N.

He prays for particular persons (if any) and continues:—

Et omnium circumstantium, quorum tibi fides cognita est, et nota devotio; pro quibus tibi offerimus, vel qui tibi offerunt, hoc sacrificium laudis; pro se suisque omnibus, pro redemptione animarum suarum, pro spe salutis, et incolumitatis suæ; tibique reddunt vota sua, æterno Deo vivo et vero.	And all here present, whose faith and devotion are known to Thee; for whom we offer to Thee or who offer to Thee this sacrifice of praise for themselves and all that belong to them, for the redemption of their souls, for the hope of their salvation and safety, and render their vows to Thee, the eternal, living and true God.

Within the "Action," or most solemn part of the Sacrifice:—

Communi- Communicating

cantes, et memoriam venerantes, imprimis gloriosæ semper Virginis Mariæ, Genitricis Dei et Domini nostri Jesu Christi, sed et beatorum Apostolorum ac Martyrum tuorum, Petri et Pauli, Andreæ, Jacobi, Joannis, Thomæ, Jacobi, Philippi, Bartholomæi, Matthæi, Simonis et Thaddæi, Lini, Cleti, Clementis, Xysti, Cornelii, Cypriani, Laurentii, Chrysogoni, Joannis et Pauli, Cosmæ et Damiani et omnium Sanctorum tuorum; quorum	and venerating the memory, in the first place, of glorious Mary ever Virgin, Mother of our Lord and God, Jesus Christ, as also of thy blessed Apostles and Martyrs, Peter and Paul, Andrew and James, John, Thomas, James, Philip, Bartholomew, Matthew, Simon and Thaddeus, Linus, Cletus, Clement, Xystus, Cornelius, Cyprian, Laurence, Chrysogonus, John and Paul, Cosmas and Damian, and all thy Saints; by whose merits and prayers mayest Thou grant, that in

meritis precibusque concedas, ut in omnibus protectionis tuæ muniamur auxilio. Per eundem Christum Dominum nostrum. Amen.

all things we may be defended by the help of thy protection. Through the same Christ our Lord. Amen.

Spreading his hands over the oblation, he says:—

Hanc igitur oblationem servitutis nostræ, sed et cunctæ familiæ tuæ, quæsumus, Domine, ut placatus accipias, diesque nostros in tua pace disponas, atque ab æterna damnatione nos eripi, et in electorum tuorum jubeas grege numerari. Per Christum Dominum nostrum. Amen.

We beseech Thee, therefore, O Lord, to receive favourably this oblation of our service, as also of all thy family; and to dispose our days in thy peace, and command us to be delivered from eternal damnation, and to be numbered in the flock of Thy elect. Through Christ our Lord. Amen.

Quam oblationem, tu, Deus, in omnibus, quæsumus benedic ✠ tam, adscrip ✠ tam, ra ✠ tam, rationabilem acceptabilemque facere digneris, ut nobis cor ✠ pus et san ✠ guis fiat dilectissimi Filii tui Domini nostri Jesu Christi.

Qui pridie quam pateretur, accepit panem in sanctas ac venerabiles manus suas, et elevatis oculis in cœlum ad te Deum Patrem suum omnipotentem, tibi gratias agens, benedixit, fregit deditque discipulis suis,

Which oblation do Thou, O God, we beseech Thee, vouchsafe to make in all things blessed, admitted, ratified, reasonable, and acceptable, that it may be made for us the Body and Blood of thy most beloved Son, Our Lord Jesus Christ.

Who, the day before He suffered, took bread into his holy and venerable hands; and, with eyes lifted up to Heaven, and to Thee, O God, his Almighty Father, giving thanks to Thee, He blessed, broke, and gave to his disciples, say-

dicens : Accipite, et manducate ex hoc omnes ;

HOC EST ENIM CORPUS MEUM.

Simili modo postquam cœnatum est, accipiens et hunc præclarum calicem in sanctas ac venerabiles manus suas, item tibi gratias agens bene ✠ dixit, deditque discipulis suis, dicens: Accipite et bibite ex eo omnes : Hic est enim Calix Sanguinis Mei Novi et Æterni Testamenti; Mysterium Fidei : qui pro vobis et pro multis effundetur in remissionem peccatorum.

ing : Take and eat you all of this;

FOR THIS IS MY BODY.

In like manner, after he had supped, taking also this excellent chalice into his holy and venerable hands, also giving thanks to Thee, He blessed it, and gave it to his disciples, saying: Take and drink ye all of this, for this is the chalice of my blood of the New and Eternal Testament, the mystery of Faith, which shall be shed for you and for many to the remission of sins.

Hæc quotiescunque feceritis, in mei memoriam facietis.	As often as you shall do these things, you shall do them in remembrance of me.
Unde et memores, Domine, nos servi tui, sed et plebs tua sancta, ejusdem Christi Filii tui Domini nostri tam beatæ passionis, necnon et ab inferis resurrectionis, sed et in cœlo gloriosæ ascensionis; offerimus præclaræ Majestati tuæ, de tuis donis ac datis, Hostiam ✠ puram, Hostiam ✠ sanctam, Hostiam ✠ immaculatam, panem ✠ sanctum vitæ æternæ, et calicem ✠ sa-	Wherefore, O Lord, we, thy servants, and likewise thy holy people, mindful as well of the blessed Passion as of the resurrection from the grave, and also the glorious ascension into Heaven, of the same Christ thy Son Our Lord, offer to Thy excellent Majesty, of thy gifts and presents, a pure victim, a holy victim, an unspotted victim, the holy bread of eternal life, and the chalice

lutis perpetuæ.	of everlasting salvation.
Supra quæ propitio ac sereno vultu respicere digneris, et accepta habere, sicuti accepta habere dignatus es munera pueri tui justi Abel, et sacrificium Patriarchæ nostri Abrahæ; et quod tibi obtulit summus sacerdos tuus Melchisedech sanctum sacrificium, immaculatam hostiam.	Upon which vouchsafe to look with a propitious and serene countenance, and accept them as thou didst vouchsafe to accept the offerings of thy just servant Abel, and the sacrifice of our patriarch Abraham, and that which thy High Priest Melchisedech offered to Thee, a holy sacrifice, an unspotted victim.

Bowing down before the Altar, he says:—

Supplices te rogamus, omnipotens Deus, jube hæc perferri per manus sancti an-	We humbly beseech thee, O Almighty God, command these things to be carried by the

geli tui in sublime altare tuum, in conspectu divinæ Majestatis tuæ: ut quotquot ex hac altaris participatione, sacrosanctum Filii tui corpus ✠ et ✠ sanguinem sumpserimus, omni benedictione cœlesti et gratia repleamur. Per eundem Christum Dominum nostrum. Amen.

hands of thy holy angel to thy altar on high, in the presence of thy Divine Majesty: that all of us who shall receive the most holy Body and Blood of thy Son, by this participation of the Altar, may be filled with all heavenly blessings and grace. Through the same Christ our Lord. Amen.

COMMEMORATION FOR THE DEAD.

Memento, etiam, Domine, famulorum famularumque tuarum, qui nos præcesserunt cum signo fidei et dormiunt in somno pacis.

Remember, also, O Lord, thy servants of both sexes, N. and N., who have gone before us with the sign of Faith, and repose in the sleep of peace.

Here he prays for particular persons (if any).

Ipsis, Domine, et omnibus in Christo quiescentibus, locum refrigerii, lucis et pacis, ut indulgeas deprecamur. Per eundem Christum, &c. Amen.	To these, O Lord, and to all who sleep in Christ, we beseech Thee to grant a place of refreshment, light and peace. Through the same Christ our Lord. Amen.

Striking his breast, and raising his voice a little:—

Nobis quoque pecatoribus,	Also to us sinners,

And continues in a low voice:—

famulis tuis de multitudine miserationum tuarum sperantibus partem aliquam et societatem donare digneris, cum tuis sanctis apostolis et martyribus ; cum Joanne, Ste-	thy servants, hoping in the multitude of thy mercies vouchsafe to grant some part and fellowship with thy holy Apostles and Martyrs; with John, Stephen, Matthias, Barna-

phano, Matthia, Barnaba, Ignatio, Alexandro, Marcellino, Petro, Felicitate, Perpetua, Agatha, Lucia, Agnete, Cæcilia, Anastasia, et omnibus sanctis tuis, intra quorum nos consortium non æstimator meriti, sed veniæ, quæsumus, largitor admitte. Per Christum Dominum nostrum Amen.

bas, Ignatius, Alexander, Marcellinus, Peter, Felicitas, Perpetua, Agatha, Lucy, Agnes, Cecilia, Anastasia, and all thy saints, into whose company do Thou, we beseech Thee, admit us, not considering our merits, but granting us thy forgiveness. Through Christ our Lord. Amen.

Per quem hæc omnia, Domine, semper bona creas, sancti ✠ ficas, vivi ✠ ficas, bene ✠ dicis, et præstas nobis. Per ip ✠ sum, et cum ip ✠ so, et

By whom, O Lord, Thou dost always create, sanctify, vivify, bless, and grant to us all these good things. Through Him, and with Him, and in Him is

in ip ✠ so, est tibi Deo Patri ✠ omnipotenti, in unitate Spiritus Sancti, omnis honor et gloria.

to Thee, O God, the Father Almighty, in the unity of the Holy Ghost, all honour and glory.

Then the Priest says aloud:—

P. Per omnia sæcula sæculorum.

P. World without end.

R. Amen.

R. Amen.

Oremus.

Let us pray.

Præceptis salutaribus moniti, et divina institutione formati, audemus dicere:

Admonished by salutary precepts, and formed by divine instruction, we presume to say:

Pater noster, qui es in cœlis, sanctificetur nomen tuum; adveniat regnum tuum; fiat voluntas tua sicut in cœlo et in terra. Panem nostrum

Our Father, who art in Heaven, hallowed be thy name; thy kingdom come; thy will be done on earth as it is in Heaven; give us this day our daily bread;

quotidianum da nobis hodie; et dimitte nobis debita nostra, sicut et nos dimittimus debitoribus nostris. Et ne nos inducas in tentationem,

R. Sed libera nos a malo.

P. Amen.

Libera nos, quæsumus, Domine, ab omnibus malis præteritis, præsentibus, et futuris: et intercedente beata et gloriosa semper Virgine Dei Genitrice Maria, cum beatis Apostolis tuis Petro et Paulo, atque Andrea et omnibus Sanctis, da pro-

and forgive us our trespasses, as we forgive them that trespass against us; and lead us not into temptation,

R. But deliver us from evil.

P. Amen.

Deliver us, we beseech thee, O Lord, from all evils, past, present, and to come; and the Blessed and glorious Mary ever Virgin, Mother of God, with thy blessed Apostles Peter and Paul, and Andrew, and all the Saints interceding, grant in thy mercy peace

pitius pacem in diebus nostris; ut ope misericordiæ tuæ adjuti, et a peccato simus semper liberi, et ab omni perturbatione securi. Per eundem Dominum nostrum Jesum Christum Filium tuum. Qui tecum vivit et regnat in unitate Spiritus Sancti Deus,

in our days; that, assisted by the help of thy mercy, we may both be ever free from sin, and secure from all disturbance. Through the same Lord Jesus Christ thy Son, who lives and reigns with Thee, in the unity of the Holy Ghost, God,

Then he says aloud:—

Per omnia sæcula sæculorum.

World without end.

R. Amen.

R. Amen.

P. Pax ✠ Domini sit ✠ semper vobis ✠ cum.

P. The peace of the Lord be always with you.

R. Et cum spiritu tuo.

R. And with thy spirit.

In a low voice:—

Hæc commixtio

May this mix-

etconsecratio corporis et sanguinis Domini nostri Jesu Christi fiat accipientibus nobis in vitam æternam. Amen.

ture and consecration of the Body and Blood of our Lord Jesus Christ be to us who receive it unto life everlasting. Amen.

Then aloud, striking his breast,

Agnus Dei, qui tollis peccata mundi, miserere nobis.

Lamb of God, who takest away the sins of the world, have mercy on us.

Agnus Dei, qui tollis peccata mundi, miserere nobis.

Lamb of God, who takest away the sins of the world, have mercy on us.

Agnus Dei, qui tollis peccata mundi, dona nobis pacem.

Lamb of God, who takest away the sins of the world, grant us peace.

Domine Jesu Christe, qui dixisti Apostolis tuis,

O Lord Jesus Christ, who didst say to thy Apostles,

pacem relinquo vobis, pacem meam do vobis; ne respicias peccata mea, sed fidem Ecclesiæ tuæ; eamque secundum voluntatem tuam pacificare et coadunare digneris. Qui vivis et regnas, Deus, per omnia sæcula sæculorum. Amen.

Domine Jesu Christe, Fili Dei vivi, qui ex voluntate Patris, cooperante Spiritu Sancto, per mortem tuam mundum vivificasti, libera me per hoc sacrosanctum corpus et sanguinem tuum ab omnibus

I leave you peace, I give you my peace; look not upon my sins but upon the faith of thy Church; and vouchsafe to pacify and unite it according to thy will. Who livest and reignest, God, world without end. Amen.

O Lord Jesus Christ, Son of the living God, who didst give life to the world by thy death, by the will of the Father and the co-operation of the Holy Ghost, deliver me by this thy most holy Body and Blood, from all

iniquitatibus meis, et universis malis; et fac me tuis semper inhærere mandatis, et a te nunquam separari permittas. Qui cum eodem Deo Patre et Spiritu Sancto vivis et regnas Deus in sæcula sæculorum. Amen.

Perceptio corporis tui, Domine Jesu Christe, quod ego indignus sumere præsumo, non mihi proveniat in judicium et condemnationem, sed pro tua pietate prosit mihi ad tutamentum mentis et corporis, et ad medelam

my iniquities and all evils, and make me ever adhere to thy commandments, and never permit me to be separated from Thee, who, with the same God the Father, and the Holy Ghost, livest and reignest God, world without end. Amen.

May the participation of thy Body, O Lord Jesus Christ, which I though unworthy presume to receive, not be to my judgment and condemnation, but in thy mercy let it avail to the safety of my soul and body, and the reception of a

percipiendam. Qui vivis et regnas cum Deo Patre, in unitate Spiritus Sancti, Deus, per omnia sæcula sæculorum. Amen.

saving remedy. Who livest and reignest with God the Father in the unity of the Holy Ghost, God, world without end. Amen.

Panem cælestem accipiam et nomen Domini invocabo.

I will take the Bread of Heaven and call upon the name of the Lord.

Then the Priest, raising his voice at the first four words, repeats three times, striking his breast :—

Domine, non sum dignus ut intres sub tectum meum, sed tantum dic verbo, et sanabitur anima mea.

Lord, I am not worthy that thou shouldst enter under my roof, but say only the word and my soul shall be healed!

After which he says :—

Corpus Domini nostri Jesu

May the Body of our Lord Jesus

Chisti custodiat animam meam in vitam æternam. Amen.

Christ preserve my soul to life eternal. Amen.

Then he receives the Host and says, after a pause :—

Quid retribuam Domino pro omnibus quæ retribuit mihi? Calicem salutaris accipiam, et nomen Domini invocabo. Laudans invocabo Dominum, et ab inimicis meis salvus ero.

What shall I return to the Lord for all that He has given to me? I will take the chalice of salvation, and call upon the name of the Lord. Praising I will call upon the Lord, and I shall be saved from my enemies.

Receiving the Chalice, he says :—

Sanguis Domini nostri Jesu Christi custodiat animam meam in vitam æternam. Amen.

May the Blood of our Lord Jesus Christ preserve my soul to life eternal. Amen.

Here Communion is administered, if there are any persons to receive it, the "Acolyte" saying the Confiteor (page 218).

The Priest turns to the people and pronounces a General Absolution in the following words:—

Misereatur vestri omnipotens Deus, et, dimissis peccatis vestris, perducat vos ad vitam æternam.	May Almighty God have mercy on you, and, your sins being forgiven, bring you to life everlasting.
R. Amen.	R. Amen.
Indulgentiam, absolutionem, et remissionem peccatorum vestrorum tribuat vobis omnipotens et misericors Dominus.	May the almighty and merciful Lord give you pardon, absolution, and remission of your sins.
R. Amen.	R. Amen.

Elevating the Blessed Sacrament, turning towards the people, he says:—

Ecce Agnus Dei; ecce qui tollit peccata mundi.	Behold the Lamb of God; behold Him who taketh away the sins of the world.

And then he repeats the "Domine, non sum dignus" three times. Coming down to the rails, he administers the Sacrament, saying to each Communicant:—

Corpus Domini nostri Jesu Christi custodiat animam tuam in vitam æternam. Amen.	May the Body of our Lord Jesus Christ preserve thy soul to life everlasting. Amen.

He returns to the altar, replaces the Ciborium in the Tabernacle, and takes wine into the chalice, saying:—

Quod ore sumpsimus, Domine, pura mente capiumus; et de munere temporali fiat nobis remedium

May we receive with a pure mind, O Lord, what we have taken with our mouth; and of a temporal gift

T

sempiternum. may it become to us an eternal remedy.

Taking wine and water into the chalice, he says:—

Corpus tuum, Domine, quod sumpsi et sanguis quem potavi adhæreat visceribus meis; et præsta ut in me non remaneat scelerum macula, quem pura et sancta refecerunt sacramenta. Qui vivis et regnas in sæcula sæculorum. Amen.

May thy Body, O Lord, which I have received, and thy Blood which I have drunk, cleave to my bowels; and grant that no stain of sin may remain in me, who have been refreshed with pure and holy sacraments. Who livest and reignest world without end. Amen.

Having covered the chalice, he goes to the book and reads the Communion, as follows:—

Communio.
Felices sensus

Happy senses of the Blessed Virgin

beatæ Mariæ Virginis, qui sine morte meruerunt martyrii palmam sub cruce Domini.

Mary, which without dying deserved the palm of martyrdom beneath the Cross of our Lord.

Turning round to the people, he says:—

P. Dominus vobiscum.
R. Et cum spiritu tuo.
Oremus.
Postcommunio.
Sacrificia quae sumpsimus, Domine Jesu Christe, transfixionem Matris tuæ et Virginis devote celebrantes, nobis impetrent apud clementiam tuam omnis boni salutaris effectum. Qui vivis, etc.

P. The Lord be with you.
R. And with thy spirit.
Let us pray.
O Lord Jesus Christ, may the sacrifice of which we have partaken in the devout celebration of the Transfixion of thy Virgin Mother, obtain for us of thy clemency, the effect of every salutary good. Who livest, etc. Amen.

The Priest turns to the people, and says:—

P. Dominus vobiscum.
P. The Lord be with you.

R. Et cum spiritu tuo.
R. And with thy spirit.

P. Ite, missa est.
P. Go, you are dismissed.

R. Deo gratias.
R. Thanks be to God.

When the "Gloria" has been omitted:—

P. Benedicamus Domino.
P. Let us bless the Lord.

R. Deo gratias.
R. Thanks be to God.

Bowing before the altar, he says:—

Placeat tibi, sancta Trinitas, obsequium servitutis meæ; et præsta, ut sacrificium quod oculis tuæ majestatis
Let the homage of my service be pleasing to Thee, O Holy Trinity, and grant that the sacrifice which I, unworthy as I am,

indignus obtuli, tibi sit acceptabile, mihique, et omnibus pro quibus illud obtuli, sit, te miserante, propitiabile. Per Christum Dominum nostrum. Amen.

have offered up in the sight of thy majesty, may be acceptable to Thee, and by thy mercy be a propitiation for me, and for all for whom I have offered it. Through Christ our Lord. Amen.

Then he gives the blessing :—

Benedicat vos omnipotens Deus, Pater et Filius ✠ et Spiritus Sanctus.
R. Amen.

May Almighty God, Father, Son, and Holy Ghost, bless you.
R. Amen.

Then follows the Gospel of St. John, if no other is to be read.

P. Dominus vobiscum.
R. Et cum spiritu tuo.

P. The Lord be with you.
R. And with thy spirit.

P. Initium sancti Evangelii secundum Joannem.

R. Gloria tibi, Domine.

In principio erat Verbum, et Verbum erat apud Deum; et Deus erat Verbum: hoc erat in principio apud Deum. Omnia per ipsum facta sunt, et sine ipso factum est nihil quod factum est: in ipso vita erat, et vita erat lux hominum; et lux in tenebris lucet, et tenebræ eam non comprehenderunt. Fuit homo missus a Deo, cui nomen erat Joannes. Hic

P. The beginning of the holy Gospel according to St. John.

R. Glory be to Thee, O Lord.

In the beginning was the Word, and the Word was with God, and the Word was God; the same was in the beginning with God. All things were made by Him, and without Him was made nothing that was made: in Him was the life, and the life was the light of men: and the light shineth in darkness, and the darkness did not comprehend it. There was a man sent from God, whose

venit in testimonium, ut testimonium perhiberet de lumine, ut omnes crederent per illum. Non erat ille lux: sed ut testimonium perhiberet de lumine. Erat lux vera quæ illuminat omnem hominem venientem in hunc mundum. In mundo erat, et mundus per ipsum factus est, et mundus eum non cognovit. In propria venit, et sui eum non receperunt. Quotquot autem receperunt eum, dedit eis potestatem filios Dei fieri; his qui credunt in nomine

name was John. This man came for a witness, to give testimony of the light, that all men might believe through him. He was not the light, but came to give testimony of the light. He was the true light which enlighteneth every man that cometh into this world. He was in the world, and the world was made by Him, and the world knew Him not. He came unto his own, and his own received Him not. But as many as received Him, to them He gave power to become

ejus, qui non ex sanguinibus, neque ex voluntate carnis, neque ex voluntate viri, sed ex Deo nati sunt. ET VERBUM CARO FACTUM EST, et habitavit in nobis; et vidimus gloriam ejus, gloriam quasi Unigeniti a Patre, plenum gratiæ et veritatis.

R. Deo gratias.

the sons of God: to those that believe in his name, who are born not of blood, nor of the will of the flesh, nor of the will of man, but of God. And the Word was made flesh, and dwelt amongst us, and we saw his glory, as it were the glory of the Only-begotten of the Father, full of grace and truth.

R. Thanks be to God.

A SHORT OFFICE

OF

The Seven Dolours

OF THE

BLESSED VIRGIN MARY.

COMPOSED BY

ST. BONAVENTURA

Translated from the Latin.

SHORT OFFICE
OF
THE SEVEN DOLOURS
OF THE
BLESSED VIRGIN MARY.

MATINS.

Hail Mary, etc.

V. O Lord, open my lips.

R. And my mouth shall declare thy praise.

V. Incline unto my aid, O God.

R. O Lord, make haste to help me.

Glory be to the, etc.

Alleluja. (During Septuag.) Praise be to Thee, O King of eternal glory.

Invitatory.

Together with the Blessed Virgin Mary, let us fervently supplicate the Lord, placed in the sepulchre.

* Come let us adore Him.

Together with the, etc.

Psalm.

Come, all ye men and women, and let us pour forth our prayers with the Blessed Virgin Mary: let us give vent to the most heartfelt wailings, and let us moisten our cheeks with our tears.

Together with the, etc.

Let our hearts fervently supplicate, and let our eyes glow from the ardour of our love: alas, the sinless Mary is deprived of so sweet a Son!

Come let us adore Him.

Innocent and sinless He dies, compassionating the human race: Oh let us be sharers in his grief, since we have been the cause of his death.

Together with the, etc.

Glory be to the Son of the Virgin Mary, who, in this exile, delivered himself up to cruel torments, in order to give back life to the miserable.

Come let us adore Him.

Together with the, etc.—Come let us adore Him.

Hymn.

I.

O Mary, my most clement Queen,
Moisten with the dews of grace
  My arid heart, that it may bring
Loving smiles to thy sweet face.

II.

Ah! grant that I may sigh with thee,
Weeping o'er the death of Him
  Whose Blood bedewed his own vast earth,
Washing it from every sin.

III.

More harshly than the vilest slave,
Jesus, thy sweet Son, is torn
  Far from thy breast, mock'd and despised,
Victim of his people's scorn.

IV.

Then let us honour, praise, and love,
Each with all the strength he can,
  Dear Mary's Son, who shed his Blood,
Dying for poor guilty man.

Antiphon.—Thou didst pass that night.

Psalm.

They have laid me in the lower pit :* in the dark places, and in the shadow of death.

Thy wrath is strong over me :* and all thy waves Thou hast brought in upon me.

Thou hast put away my acquaintance far from me :* they have set me in abomination to themselves.

I was delivered up and came not forth :* my eyes languished through poverty.

Glory be to the Father, etc.

Antiphon.—Thou didst pass that night in which Christ was taken, without sleep ; and whilst the others slept in the midst of their grief, thou alone, O Mary, didst not sleep, but remainedst sorrowfully watching.

V. The others slept in the midst of their weepings.

R. But thou alone didst keep the sorrowful vigils.

Our Father (in secret).

V. Lead us not into temptation.
R. But deliver us from evil.

Absolution.—Do not leave me, my dear Jesus, but grant that by a like passion I may die with Thee.
R. Amen.
V. Pray, Sir, a blessing.
Blessing.—O beautiful Virgin, pray for us to Jesus crucified.
R. Amen.

Lesson I.

The sorrowful Mother gazes fixedly upon her Son hanging upon the cross, and weeps incessantly. Striking her sacred breast she moves many to tears by her bitter grief, as she looks upon her bleeding Son, stretched upon the gibbet of the cross. Then it was, alas, that, according to the prediction of Simeon, a sharp sword of sorrow pierced the heart of the weeping Mother. And while she thus deplores the death of her offspring, her only consoler was St. John, who was her guardian, and Jesus' disciple.

But Thou, O Lord, have mercy on us.

R. Thanks be to God.

V. The Mother could not be consoled, seeing her Son thus so cruelly treated.

R. None but our Saviour, who suffered so much, endured such bitter grief.

V. Seeing the death of the God she had nourished, Mary grieved more than ever any other mother.

R. None but our Saviour, &c.

V. Pray, Sir, a blessing.

Blessing.—May the death of the Son of God the Father be our life, through the prayers of the most pious Mother Mary. R. Amen.

Lesson II.

When Jesus was taken down from the cross, and was being carried to the tomb, his sorrowful mother, in an agony of grief, thus addressed the bearers of his body: "Wait here a little, that I may grieve over his sufferings, and may kiss my most beloved one. Ah! do not take from me so dear, so amiable a Son. If He must be buried, then bury me along with Him." Then, exhausted by suffering and grief, she approaches, throws herself upon his Body, and moistens his sacred countenance with her tears.

But Thou, O Lord, have mercy on us.
R. Thanks be to God.
V. Whilst she witnesses the cruel tortures of her Son, her Immaculate heart is wrung with overwhelming grief, and during those three long days that she languished from suffering,
R. Her face became ghastly pale, lately so beautiful.
V. Torture so exquisite was never yet heard of; far more preferable to her was death than life.
R. Her face became, etc.
V. Pray, Sir, a blessing.

Blessing.—May the most chaste Virgin Mother be our peacemaker at the throne of the Omnipotent. Amen.

Lesson III.

The Mother, now deprived of her Son's presence, thus speaks to the Angel Gabriel:—"'Hail, full of grace,' were the words which you once said to me; but behold, now I am full of bitter grief! And, again, you told me that 'the Lord is with thee;' but, alas! He lies buried in the tomb, and is no longer with me. All the blessings which you once promised me are now turned into sorrows by the death of my Jesus."

But Thou, O Lord, have mercy on us.
R. Thanks be to God.
V. When the tomb was closed and the Body of Jesus was hidden from Mary's view,
R. The sorrows of her heart became still more intense.
V. By the gushing stream of her tears she causes those also to weep who stood around.
R. The sorrows of her, etc.
V. Glory be to the, etc.
R. The sorrows of her, etc.

LAUDS.

Incline unto my aid, O God, etc.
Ant. The voice of the Mother.

Psalm.

But I am a worm and no man :* the reproach of men and an outcast of the people.

All they that saw me have laughed me to scorn :* they have spoken with the lips and wagged the head.

He hoped in the Lord, let Him deliver Him :* let Him save Him, seeing He delighteth in Him.

For Thou art He that hast drawn me out of the womb :* my hope from the breast of my Mother, I was cast upon Thee from the womb.

Glory be to the Father, etc.

Ant. The voice of the Mother becomes sorrowful and sad, now that her beloved Son is taken from her.

The Little Chapter.

When the Virgin Mary heard that her Son was taken from her by the

Jews, and led to Annas, she shut herself up in her chamber, struck her sacred breast, and gave herself up to incessant weeping.

R. Thanks be to God.

Hymn.

I.

O glorious Queen! to what a height
   Thy agonies increased!
When Jesus was condemned to death!
   And Barabbas was released.

II.

They strike the Shepherd! Then, alas!
   The sheep all scattered fly;
But thou remainest with St. John,
   To see thy Jesus die.

III.

No wonder, then, that thou shouldst be
   A mark for Satan's scorn;
Since from thy sacred womb, great Queen,
   Th' Incarnate Word was born.

IV.

Then let us honour, praise, and love,
 With all the strength we can,
Dear Mary's Son, who shed his Blood,
 To save poor sinful man. Amen.

V. Never has a Mother suffered such overwhelming grief,

R. As Mary, when she gazed upon the cruel tortures of her Son.

Ant. Like a thief he was assaulted.

Canticle of Zachary.

Blessed be the Lord God of Israel : * because He hath visited and wrought the redemption of his people.

And hath raised up a horn of salvation to us :* in the house of David his servant.

As he spoke by the mouth of his holy Prophets :* who are from the beginning.

Salvation from our enemies :* and from the hand of all that hate us.

To perform mercy to our fathers :* and to remember his holy testimony.

The oath which He swore to Abraham our father :* that He would grant to us.

That being delivered from the hand of our enemies :* we may serve Him without fear.

In holiness and justice before Him :* all our days.

And thou, child, shalt be called the prophet of the Highest :* for thou shalt go before the face of the Lord, to prepare his ways.

To give knowledge of salvation to his people:* unto the remission of sins.

Through the bowels of the mercy of our God :* in which the Orient from on high hath visited us.

To enlighten them that sit in darkness and in the shadow of death :* to direct our feet into the way of peace.

Glory be to the Father, etc.

Ant. Like a thief he was assaulted, borne away, and cruelly beaten, spat upon and buffeted. Oh! immense grief of the Mother, when she heard those heavy, dreadful blows! Blessed be our King who bore such things for us.

V. O Lord, hear my prayer.
R. And let my cry come unto Thee.

Let us pray.

By those terrible sufferings which tortured thy sacred heart, O my most amiable Mother! when thou didst hear that thy beloved Son was carried off by impious men, bound and led away to death, assist us, that our hearts may be terrified at our iniquities, and moved to penance, lest at the hour of death we be terrified at the assaults of the Evil One, and being accused by our own guilty consciences, be filled with consternation at the aspect of the tremendous Judge; and grant us thy help and protection that, on the contrary, seeing his face, our hearts may be filled with great joy and ineffable delight. Through Jesus Christ thy Son, who with the Father and the Holy Ghost lives and reigns, God, world without end. Amen.

PRIME.

Hail Mary, etc. V. Incline unto my aid, etc.

Hymn.

I.

O Jesus, fruit of Mary's womb,
    Of Jesse's mystic tree,
Who torn and bruised, for sinners died,
    In silent agony.

II.

Oh! by thy love for her sad heart,
    Let our sins be forgiven,
And let the stream of Mary's tears
    Give easy course to Heaven.

III.

Then let us honour, praise, and love,
    With all the strength we can,
Dear Mary's Son, who shed his Blood,
    To save poor sinful man. Amen.
Ant. The most pious Virgin.

Psalm.

The kings of the earth stood up, and the princes met together :* against the Lord, and against his Christ.

Let us break their bonds asunder :* and let us cast away their yoke from us.

He that dwelleth in Heaven shall laugh at them :* and the Lord shall deride them.

Then shall He speak to them in his anger :* and trouble them in his rage.

Glory be to the Father, etc.

Ant. The most pious Virgin remained within the solitude of her chamber, weeping bitterly, whilst the furious Jews seized and dragged away the King of the world.

The Little Chapter.

May the stream of thy tears flow in upon our stony hearts, and cause them to grieve sincerely.

R. Thanks be to God.

V. By the tears of Mary, O Father of piety,

R. Confer upon us that glory which the blessed enjoy.

Let us Pray.

By those heartrending sighs and

tears which thy breast could not restrain, O my most sweet Mother! when thou didst behold thy dearest Son presented to the impious judge, most cruelly scourged and exposed to mockery and insult for our sins; obtain for us a deep sorrow and tears of salutary contrition for our iniquities; help us by thy gracious assistance, so that the devil may not have power to deceive us and put us to shame, and that we ourselves may not give way to his frequent solicitations to sin, or have to stand one day, conquered and overcome, in the presence of the tremendous Judge. But that, on the contrary, we may accuse ourselves sincerely now, and judge ourselves for our excesses, and may so scourge ourselves with the rod of penance as to obtain pardon and grace during these times of suffering, tribulation, and distress, through our Lord Jesus Christ, who lives and reigns with the Father and the Holy Ghost, God, world without end. Amen.

Tierce.

Hail Mary, etc. Incline unto my aid, etc.

Hymn.

O Jesus, fruit of Mary's womb, etc.

Ant. Oh! how great was Mary's grief.

Psalm.

Because for thy sake I have borne reproach :* shame hath covered my face.

I am become a stranger to my brethren :* and am an alien to the sons of my mother.

For the zeal of thy house hath eaten me up :* and the reproaches of them that reproached Thee are fallen upon me.

And I covered my soul in fasting :* and it was made a reproach to me.

Glory be to the Father, etc.

Ant. Oh! how great was Mary's grief when she beheld that of her Son. There is no sorrow like unto that of the Virgin Mary weeping over the passion of Him who is both God and Man.

The Little Chapter.

Whilst Christ was being led to Calvary and was bearing his cross thither, his Mother followed, sighing and weeping most pitifully, shedding abundance of tears, and striking her sacred breast.

R. Thanks be to God.

V. I beseech thee, O Queen of Virgins,

R. To obtain for me the favour of sharing in thy grief.

V. O Lord, hear my prayer, etc.

Let us Pray.

By those excruciating sufferings which thy heart underwent, most Blessed Virgin, when thou didst hear that thy Son was condemned to death and to the ignominy of the cross, help us in the time of our weakness, especially when our bodies shall be loaded with infirmities, and our spirit disturbed on one side by the snares of the demons and on the other by the terrible aspect of the most just and avenging Judge. Help us then, O dear Lady, we implore thee, lest the sentence of our eternal damnation be passed upon us and we thus be eternally condemned to the flames of hell. Through Jesus Christ, thy Son, who with the Father and the Holy Ghost lives and reigns world without end Amen.

Sext.

Hail Mary, etc. Incline unto my aid, etc.

Hymn.

O Jesus, fruit of Mary's womb (as at Prime).

Ant. When the Blessed Virgin arrives.

Psalm.

My strength is dried up like a potsherd, and my tongue hath cleaved to my jaws :* and Thou has brought me down into the dust of the earth.

For many dogs have encompassed me :* the council of the malignant hath besieged me.

They have dug my hands and feet :* they have numbered all my bones.

And they have looked and stared upon me, they have parted my garments amongst them :* and upon my vesture they cast lots.

Glory be to the Father, etc.

Ant. When the Blessed Virgin arrives at the place of punishment, as soon as she sees her Son and his cross, her sighs and tears increase, her sorrows and sufferings are multiplied.

The Little Chapter.

Already doth Jesus extend his hands and feet. Behold, now they are nailed to the cross, and the cross is raised! At this sad sight the Mother fainted away with grief.

R. Thanks be to God.

V. Mary, who was like a blooming rose, faded and changed, alas! to the colour of death.

R. When she saw the sacred Blood trickle down upon the ground.

V. O Lord, hear my prayer, etc.

Let us pray.

By that sword of sorrow which pierced thy soul, O most tender Virgin, when thou didst behold thy most tender Son raised aloft, naked, upon the Cross, pierced with a lance, and lacerated throughout all his members with blows, stripes, and wounds, assist us, that our hearts may now be transfixed with the sword of contrition and compunction, and wounded with the lance of love; so that all the corrupted blood of sin may issue forth from our breasts, and that we may be cleansed from iniquity, clothed in the garment of virtue, and raised in mind and body to those delights in which we hope fully to participate when the promised day arrives. Through Jesus Christ thy Son, who with the Father and the Holy Ghost lives and reigns, God, world without end. Amen.

NONE.

Hail, Mary, etc. Incline unto my aid, etc.

Hymn.

O Jesus, fruit of Mary's womb, (as at Prime).

Ant. Jesus, like a meek lamb.

Psalm.

Thou knowest my reproach and my confusion :* and my shame.

In thy sight are all they that afflict me :* my heart hath expected reproach and misery.

I looked for one that would grieve together with me, but there was none :* and for one that would comfort me, and I found none.

And they gave me gall for my food :* and in my thirst they gave me vinegar to drink.

Glory be to the Father, etc.

Ant. Jesus, like a meek lamb, bowing his head, cries out upon the Cross with his dying voice, "Eli! Eli!" At this cry, Mary sighed, and almost fainted away.

The Little Chapter.

The cry of Jesus fills the Mother

with the greatest grief: she cannot restrain her gushing tears; both are distressed at one another's sufferings, for they love one another with the greatest love.

R. Thanks be to God.

V. O Virgin Mother, render by thy prayers,

R. Thy crucified Son propitious to the miserable.

V. O Lord, hear my prayer, etc.

Let us pray.

By the grief and anguish with which thy heart was tortured, O most sacred Mother, when, standing near the Cross, thou didst hear thy Son cry out with a loud voice, from his excessive torments, and when, after having given thee into the care of St. John, He gave up his Spirit into the hands of God the Father, help us, we beseech thee, at the end of our lives, especially at that awful moment when our tongues shall cleave to our jaws, unable to invoke thy holy name; when our eyes shall be deprived of light, when our ears shall no longer have the power of hearing, and when, in fine, all our senses shall become useless. Remember, then, O most sweet Lady, how we now pour forth our prayers in thy clement and attentive ear. Help us in that hour of extreme necessity, and recommend us to thy most beloved Son, that by Him we may, through thy intercession, be snatched from all pains and torments, and be safely conducted to the long-desired repose of the celestial country. Amen.

VESPERS.

Hail, Mary, etc. Incline unto my aid, etc.

Ant. Let every age.

Psalm.

Save me, O God!* for the waters have come in even unto my soul.

I stick fast in the mire of the deep: * and there is no sure standing.

I am come into the depths of the sea:* and a tempest hath overwhelmed me.

I have laboured with crying, my jaws are become hoarse:* my eyes have failed whilst I hoped in my God.

Glory be to the Father, etc.

Ant. Let every age mourn over the death of the Saviour, and over the heart of his virginal Mother, transpierced with a sword of sorrow.

The Little Chapter.

Be it far from me that I should glory, save in the Cross of our Lord Jesus Christ, by whom the world is crucified to me and I to the world.

R. Thanks be to God.

Hymn.

I.

How saddened was dear Mary's heart,
   How thickly grew her gloom,
When ruffian hands so harshly bruised
The fruit of her blest womb.

II.

They push, they strike, they spit upon
   Her panting, bleeding Son;

She hears the blows, she sees the
    blood,
  She faints, by grief undone!

III.

And when to death He's dragged
    away,
  The Mother follows, too;
Her heart is tortured with her Son's;
  Were ever hearts so true?

IV.

Ah! now He hangs upon the cross,
  And Mary stands beside,
And prays for us with breaking heart,
  To Jesus crucified.

V.

Then let us honour, praise, and love,
  With all the strength we can,
Dear Mary's Son, who shed his Blood
  To save poor sinful man.

V. No mother ever endured such torments as Mary.

R. When she saw the large bleeding wounds in the head of her Son.

Ant. When our Lord was dead.

Canticle of the Blessed Virgin Mary.

My soul * doth magnify the Lord.

And my spirit * hath rejoiced in God my Saviour.

Because He hath regarded the humility of his handmaid :* for behold from henceforth all generations shall call me blessed.

Because He that is mighty hath done great things to me :* and holy is his name.

And his mercy is from generation unto generations :* to them that fear Him.

He hath showed might in his arm :* He hath scattered the proud in the conceit of their hearts.

He hath put down the mighty from their seat :* and hath exalted the humble.

He hath filled the hungry with good things :* and the rich He hath sent away empty.

He hath received Israel his servant :* being mindful of his mercy,

As he spoke to our fathers :* to Abraham and his seed for ever.

Glory be to the Father, etc.

Ant. When our Lord was dead the Blessed Virgin's grief became still more manifest to the surrounding people; and sorrowfully did she sigh and supplicate in the intensity of her grief, with that same voice which once had sung in such joyful strains, " Magnificat."

V. O Lord, hear my prayer, etc.

Let us pray.

By the wailings of thy sweet voice which thou, most chaste Virgin, wert not able to contain within the gushing fountain of thy breast, when, as is piously believed, thou didst rush forward to embrace the dead body of thy Son, taken down from the cross, whose once beautiful and radiant face thou didst then behold covered with the paleness of death; whose wounded and lacerated body thou didst sorrowfully gaze upon ; grant us, we beseech thee, that we may now deplore our sins, and so entirely cure, by the salutary medicine of penance, our numberless iniquities, that when our bodies shall be dead, our souls may shine forth with the lustre of innocence; that thus we may be found worthy to gaze upon thy enrapturing eyes, and be encompassed in thy loving embraces, and especially in the embraces of thy most sweet Son, Jesus Christ, who, with the Father and the Holy Ghost, lives and reigns God, world without end. Amen.

COMPLIN.

V. Incline unto my aid, etc.
Ant. May the sufferings of Mary.

Psalm.

All my enemies whispered together against me :* they devised evils to me.

They determined against me an unjust word :* shall he that sleepeth rise again no more?

For even the man of my peace in whom I trusted :* who eat my bread, hath greatly supplanted me.

But Thou, O Lord, have mercy on me, and raise me up again :* and I will requite them.

Glory be to the Father, etc.

Ant. May the sufferings of Mary, O great King Jesus, preserve us from the eternal flames of hell.

Hymn.

I.

O Mary! what o'erwhelming grief,
   Burst o'er thee, like a sea,
When Jesus, thy Almighty Son,
   Was torn away from thee.

II.

Loud were thy sighs and heart-heav'd
      groans,
   As dolefully you wept,
And 'neath the Temple's silent roof
   Thy lonely vigils kept.

III.

Then let us honour, praise, and love,
   With all the strength we can,
Dear Mary's Son who shed his Blood,
   To save poor sinful man.

The Little Chapter.

Jesus being now buried, and the disciples all dispersed, the faith of the Universal Church remained only in the Mother of Jesus Christ.

R. Thanks be to God.

V. After the death of her Son, the Blessed Virgin remained with St. John.

R. Prepared for imprisonment or death.

Ant. The sword of sorrow.

Canticle of Simeon.

Now Thou dost dismiss thy servant, O Lord :* according to thy word, in peace.

Because my eyes* have seen thy salvation.

Which Thou hast prepared* before the face of all people.

A light to the revelation of the Gentiles : * and the glory of thy people Israel.

Glory be to the Father, etc.

Ant. The sword of sorrow, O Immaculate Virgin! has pierced thy heart with all the bitterness which Simeon predicted, when, full of the Holy Spirit, he said, "Now Thou dost dismiss thy servant, O Lord."

V. O Lord, hear my prayer, etc.

Let us pray.

By the sighs and groans, and indescribable grief which overwhelmed thy Immaculate Heart, O most glorious Virgin, when thou didst see thine only-begotten Son, the solace of thy soul, taken from thee, and buried in the sepulchre, turn thine eyes of mercy towards us exiles and sons of Eve, crying unto thee and sighing sorrowfully in this valley of tears, and after this our exile, show unto us the blessed fruit of thy womb, Jesus, and obtain for us by thy supplications, that we may be strengthened by the Sacraments of the Church, and die happily, and then be mercifully presented to our Eternal Judge. Through the same Lord Jesus Christ, thy Son, who with the Father and the Holy Ghost lives and reigns God, world without end. Amen.

V. O Lord, hear my prayer, etc.

O Holy Mary, Mother of Dolours, by the sword of sorrow which pierced thy soul, pray for us to the Divine Son, and obtain for us also the fruit of his Sacred Passion, now, and in the hour of our death. Amen.

May the divine assistance remain always with us. Amen.

Our Father. Hail Mary. I believe.

Write, O sweet Lady, thy wounds in my heart, that I may read in them thy sorrow and thy love—thy sorrow, that I may suffer all sorrow for thee; thy love, that I may contemn all other love for Jesus and for thee.

Praise be to God.

And to the Immaculate Heart of Mary, pierced by many swords of sorrow.

A DEVOTION

TO THE

COMPASSIONATE HEART OF MARY.

The object of this devotion is twofold; first, to honour the Most Holy Heart of Mary, suffering during her whole life—but particularly while at the foot of the cross of her Divine Son—exquisite interior torments for the salvation of souls. Second, to obtain, through this dolorous compassion, the grace of conversion for all sinners, especially those, who, by their bad example and pernicious doctrine, cause others to fall into sin.

Prayer to be said daily.

O clementissima Maria, refugium peccatorum, obsecro te per dolores Cordis tui	O most merciful Mary, refuge of sinners, I entreat thee, by the sufferings of thy most

compassione pleni, et per mortem dilecti Filii tui Jesu, impetra omnibus peccatoribus mundi, iis præsertim qui scandalis et pravis doctrinis alios in peccatum inducunt, gratiam ut sincere convertantur. Amen.

Cor Mariæ compatiens, succurre peccatoribus.

compassionate Heart, and by the death of thy beloved Son, Jesus, to obtain the grace of sincere conversion for all sinners, particularly for those who, by their scandals and wicked doctrine, draw others into sin. Amen.

O compassionate Heart of Mary, convert these sinners.

Practice.

Offer to the compassionate Heart of Mary, with this prayer, some of the actions of the day, for the conversion of all sinners throughout the world.

RULE OF LIFE.

1. Endeavour to have a good intention in all you do; for since the intention is the eye of the soul, if that be correct, your whole life will be correct.

2. No virtue is sound without real humility; never, therefore, speak in your own praise, nor against yourself—both are equally dangerous.

3. Mystics tell us there is such a thing as false humility. We must believe them. Therefore, be careful to avoid pretended humility.

4. There are two kinds of humility—humility of intellect, and humility of will. Strive, each day, to practice both. Humility of the intellect is a frank, honest, and fair acknowedgment of our total dependence on God, and of our real incapability of doing anything good without

his assistance. Humility of the will is the readiness of the heart to suffer patiently all the crosses, sorrows, and mortifications of life, because we deserve them for our sins.

5. It is not pride to think we have talents, if we thank God for them, and use them for his honour and glory; but it is more prudent to think very little of personal gifts. Therefore, always endeavour to do your best, and leave the rest to God.

6. The only thing which we can claim as our own is sin—everything else comes from Heaven: often, then, call to mind how little you have loved God.

7. If you cannot speak well of people do not speak at all of them.

8. Speak well of everybody, and always believe that he has a good intention in his doings; but if his actions are really wrong, put them down to his ignorance.

9. Be kind, affable, and gentle to all, but more especially to enemies and the poor.

10. Be severe and austere to yourself if you like, but never be harsh with others.

11. People living in the world should neither dress above their station and means, nor too much beneath their position in society.

12. Never argue with any one; but for the sake of peace, let people keep their own opinion, as you love to follow yours.

13. In matters of religion, never be ashamed of your faith, but always study to avoid all controversies—they do no good to either party.

14. Instruct others if they will listen to you; but never allow them to contend with you.

15. Bear very patiently the whims, fancies, ways, and sins of those with whom you live—remember they have to bear all your faults and peculiarities.

16. Never be gloomy or sad, but, keeping yourself always in God's presence, strive to be at all times cheerful, happy, and gay.

17. Over and over again during the day, look up to Heaven, and make some very fervent and pious ejaculations.

18. Often repeat this one: "Jesus, I love Thee; teach me to love Thee daily more and more."

19. Morning, noon, and night, make a spiritual communion, with very great devotion of heart.

20. Approach to the Holy Altar as often as possible. It is a mistake to think you can go too frequently, when you have leave from your confessor.

21. Rise early in the morning, and retire early every night.

22. As soon as you awake, thank God for his blessings during the night; offer him your heart, and consecrate to him your every faculty—all that you do, and all that you will go through during the course of the day.

23. Whilst dressing, meditate on the Passion in the following way: 1st. Whilst arranging the hair, think how the sacred head of Jesus was surrounded and penetrated with

thorns. 2nd. If you use the glass, think how the face of your only true Lover was bruised, torn, and defiled with phlegm and blood; and his eyes were suffused and bedimmed with tears and blood. 3rd. While adjusting your dress, think how cruelly Jesus was scourged at the pillar—his bones were laid bare, so that they could be counted—and think how He was dressed up in derision as a mock king, with a ragged purple garment. 4th. When you put on your shoes, reflect that Jesus had nothing whatever on his wounded feet, and call to mind how very much they were broken and torn, when he walked up the rugged heights of Calvary. 5th. In washing, remember how Pontius Pilate washed his guilty hands in the innocent blood of Jesus.

24. Meditate, every morning, for at least a quarter of an hour, on some particular stage of our Lord's sacred Passion, or the Dolours of the Blessed Virgin Mary. Attend Mass every day, if possible.

25. Twice in the day make spiritual reading for at least five minutes.

26. Every night say the Rosary or some litany.

27. In bed, place your arms in the form of a cross; put yourself under the special care of your guardian angel and the most sure protection of Mary Immaculate, and then offer your heart and slumbers to God Almighty.

SEPTEMBER.

The Month of Devotion

TO THE SUFFERING HEART OF MARY,

To obtain, through her Seven Dolours, the grace of Perfect Conformity to the Will of God.

MEDITATION.—*On Mary's affliction when Jesus came to ask her consent that He should die.*

FIRST POINT.

Contemplate the Lord Jesus on the eve of his departure for the accomplishment of his much-desired Passion, coming to take a last farewell of his tenderly loved and most loving mother. He is not now going merely for forty days into a desert; He goes to complete that journey to Calvary which He began, we may say, in the Garden of Paradise, when He offered Himself a victim, and promised for his mother that she should crush the serpent's head. From the gory cross will she hear his sweet voice once more. The death of a son is usually broken by friends to the parents, but this heroic Child offers Himself to die for his brethren, and He will first, like a dutiful son, get his parent's consent in so important an affair. Mother, He says, I am going to die, my Father has given me orders to that effect, but I wish also to have your permission. Maternal love would fain say, Oh, not so, my son; but, with tears of agony, her resignation to her Heavenly Father's will elicits from her words to this effect— Yes, yes, go my son, go and die. What heroic detachment this! In what do you imitate it?

SECOND POINT.

Perhaps you are so attached to that world which crucified Jesus that you will not sacrifice that insatiable desire which secretly preys upon your soul, of pleasing creatures, and yielding to every strong inclination that you do not consider absolutely sinful. Will you ask the world's permission to mortify yourself and to leave it, that you may seek God's will alone. If you do, it will always find some pretext to make you wait awhile. Do you want to kill yourself, to make yourself singular? Ah, the world is the enemy of God: make no compromise with it; you must treat it roughly and decidedly, and never again look back. Conform for God as far as duty requires but no more.

Aspiration.

O Mother of Sorrows, conceived without sin, imprint deeply on all hearts the wounds of Jesus and thy Dolours.

300 days' indulgence. To be said seven times with seven Hail Marys; a plenary, if said daily for a month.

Practice.

Seven Hail Marys with arms extended in the form of the Cross.

Patron.—St. Paul of the Cross.

SEPTEMBER.

The Month of the Seven Dolours.

I. It would be well on awaking in the morning, to go in spirit to Calvary and present your heart to this sweet, suffering Mother, that she may place it within the burning Heart of her Divine Son, and obtain for you the gifts and fruits of the Holy Ghost, thereby worthily to venerate and sympathize with her and with that Adorable Victim in their mysterious sorrows.

II. Be mindful to unite each pain of mind or body with those unparalleled woes it was her lot to endure in the great work of man's redemption. Thank her, when her maternal providence sends you a portion of the Cross of her Divine Son and of her own—the greatest mark of her protecting love, and say with a Xavier, and with all her true children : "*Yet more, sweet Mother, yet more.*" Ask true *patience* for me, that with thee I may say with truth, "*Behold the handmaid of the Lord: be it done unto me according to thy word.*"

PRAYER.

O soul-stricken martyr, whose sufferings were veiled in the same silence and humility as the surpassing holiness of thy life, obtain for us the grace of sanctifying our trials and sufferings by patient silence and conformity with God's blessed will—desiring neither the comfort nor applause of creatures, but seeking all our light, courage, and strength in the bosom of our Heavenly Father and in the tender and compassionate Hearts of Jesus, Mary, and Joseph. We offer up all our actions of this month, together with all the Masses that are being now celebrated and will be celebrated to the end of time, to Honour the Sacred Passion of Jesus and the Sorrows of Mary; and to obtain conversion for all sinners, and for ourselves and all fellow-christians the grace of perfect conformity to God's blessed will.

Great indulgences (especially at the hour of death) for reciting often the following aspiration : "*May the most just and holy will of God be accomplished in all things, and praised, and glorified for ever.*"—Amen.

Example.

At Florence, a ferocious lion escaped from the menagerie. He ran through the streets, exciting terror and confusion by his terrible roaring, and threatening carnage and destruction. He suddenly stopped outside the church of the Servites. Not knowing how to confine him, the inhabitants were afraid to stir out of their houses. A Servite brother inspired by God came out of his convent alone and unarmed, and walked with great intrepidity up to the lion, whilst invoking with a lively faith the aid of the Mother of Sorrows, when, to the surprise of all, he made the animal stand still, and put his habit about its neck. The lion became as gentle as a lamb, and allowed himself to be led back to his cage amidst the benedictions of the people.

www.ingramcontent.com/pod-product-compliance
Lightning Source LLC
Chambersburg PA
CBHW022021240426
43667CB00042B/1044